A PATH TO
Financial
Peace of Mind

Dwayne Burnell, MBA

FinancialBallGame.com

ISBN 978-0-98413-350-5
Library of Congress Number: 2009942555
Personal Finance, Investments, Life Insurance

A Path to Financial Peace of Mind
By Dwayne Burnell, MBA

FinancialBallGamePublishing.com
PO Box 1089
Bothell, WA 98041
DwayneBurnell@FinancialBallGame.com
www.FinancialBallGame.com
800-266-2971 (toll free)
425-286-7298

Printed in the United States of America

10 9 8 7 6 5 4 3 2 1

Book design by DesignForBooks.com
Cover photo by iStock©piskunov

Contents

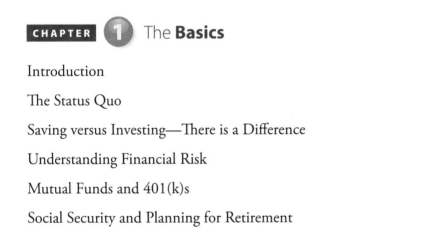

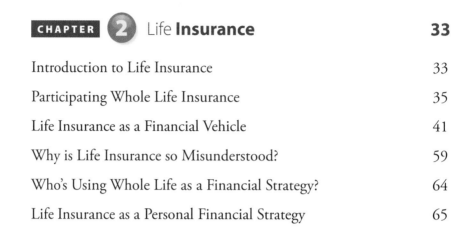

Foreword

Over the last ten years, many people have reported back to me how my book, *Becoming Your Own Banker*™—*The Infinite Banking Concept*™, has changed their lives. But none seem to have grasped the depth of what I'm teaching better than Dwayne Burnell. He does an excellent job of describing why participating whole life insurance is a phenomenal financial tool in which to build and store wealth today and for the future.

My initial Bachelors Degree is in Forestry and that background helped me to learn the value of thinking "long range." I tend to think about what will be happening 70 years from now. I'm not going to be here—and maybe neither will you—but there is certainly no harm in thinking that way. With that in mind, Dwayne quotes a line from my book, "Plan as if you are going to live forever and live as if you are going to die today."

Businesses come and go. Technology changes the way we live and behave. But the concept of using participating whole life as part of a financial strategy has been around for a long, long time. Over the years, people have abandoned their financial responsibility and accountability to themselves and have turned it over to the "experts." As of the date of this book you can clearly see the tragedy of relying on the "experts."

Dwayne Burnell has created the strongest case study illustrating *The Infinite Banking Concept*™ view point I have seen to date. In this book, *A Path to Financial Peace of Mind*, Dwayne effectively describes how to use life insurance and specifically why participating whole life insurance is so powerful for everyday living.

Dwayne has done a fantastic job of stimulating the imagination of readers and showing them a way out of the financial prison in which most folks live.

R. Nelson Nash
Becoming Your Own Banker™—
The Infinite Banking Concept™

Preface

Financial information is endlessly available to us but where shall wisdom be found? If you are fortunate, you encounter a particular teacher or set of teachers who can help you. This is what happened to me.

I'd had twenty-plus years of business experience in small and large corporations, successfully started and operated my own businesses and returned to school for an MBA in my early forties. Up to that time, I had only heard and followed the conventional financial wisdom about investing in 401(k)s, diversifying risk, and riding out rough economic times by staying in the stock market.

Then I read R. Nelson Nash's book, *Becoming Your Own Banker*™— *The Infinite Banking Concept*™, and my world changed. It was that dramatic! I started to realize the empowerment of participating whole life insurance as a key element to financial stability, and as a means to create wealth for myself and my family for generations to come.

I marveled and wondered that through all my business ventures, discussions with financial gurus over the years, and all the classes with top business university faculty, no one ever presented the value and inherent good sense of using a carefully designed participating whole life insurance policy as a financial tool. Why? The strategy isn't new. Banks, corporations, and the wealthy have long known and used the permanent whole life insurance contract to create and grow their wealth. Why is it that this powerful financial tool isn't well known or used by the general public?

I'm still working toward an answer to that question. However, I think a partial answer might be that there are powerful forces in place to keep the stock market at the forefront of our financial thinking. Two of these forces are the "mutual fund industry" and Wall Street. Another is simply the result of constantly hearing and reading on a daily basis that we must be in the market and just "buy and hold" to see our money grow. You can always count on conventional wisdom to be conventional, but it's not guaranteed to be wise.

The chief purpose of this book is to take a closer look at the value of permanent whole life insurance. Specifically, I will examine participating (i.e., dividend-paying) permanent whole life insurance as a fundamental financial tool and an effective, lifelong strategy in managing your money and your wealth.

To really absorb the information presented in this book, you'll need to be open to seeing the financial world from a different perspective. Remember, it's more than likely that stereotypical financial wisdom has taken you to where you are today. This could be a good thing. However, if, like many of us, you're concerned about leaving your money in the stock market and hoping that your stocks or mutual funds recover in time to pay for college or fund your retirement, know that there is a better, more sane way to manage your financial resources.

If you want to learn how to take ownership of your finances and your financial future, then this book is for you.

— Dwayne Burnell, MBA

Acknowledgments

I have many people to thank.

R. Nelson Nash and David Stearns planted the seeds for this book. It has been a real honor and pleasure working with both Nelson and David throughout the writing of this book. I owe R. Nelson Nash sincere thanks for his book, *Becoming Your Own Banker*™—*The Infinite Banking Concept*™, as reading this book marked a true turning point in my financial knowledge.

I am deeply grateful to Donald L. Blanton for the insight and knowledge he provided with his Money*Trax* software and the Circle of Wealth® philosophy. With these materials, I have learned how to look at personal financial management with a new perspective and passion.

I owe much to L. Ross Van Houten, my friend and colleague. Over our years of friendship, he has proven to be a wealth of financial knowledge, humor, and insight.

While the bulk of my early writing didn't find its way into the final version of this project, the knowledge I gained from the conversations I had over the years with the following people helped shape the course and direction of this book. My sincere thanks to Ray Poteet, David Cobb, LeRoy Lopez, Leonard Renier, Terry O'Brien, Rich Keal and Dr. Tomas McFie.

In the various stages of this project, many friends and colleagues read manuscripts and offered valuable criticism and conversation. My thanks to John Baker, Kirk Bradley, Ellen Breiten, David Francis, John Harding, Joe Kane, Lori Lawson, Karly Leyde, Dan Munro, Sal Petruzzella, Bobby Rice, Rebecca Rice, David Richert, Anthony Robinson, Shelly Rocha, Cathy Rose, Jim Rose, Ted Therriault and John Uttz.

I appreciate Carlos Rocha's steadfast encouragement, generous administrative support and careful review of draft manuscripts.

Kelly Lawson provided tremendous computer and editorial support, dragging me into the Twenty-first Century world of Google docs and iPhones. Kelly also demonstrated a remarkable capacity to maintain her sense of humor and direction no matter what came her way.

Brian Leyde has been a co-presenter at numerous financial educational seminars. I appreciate the depth of his tax expertise and the humor that he brought along with it.

I thank Dr. Kevin J. Lasko, Jonhenri Ball, Sean McIvor, Susan Miller, Lee Myers, Diane Paynton and Laura Eskildsen for their support.

Michael Rohani provided skillful book design and publishing expertise.

Andrea Howe provided helpful direction for the book with her professional editing of the first draft.

I would also like to acknowledge the professors and instructors in the MBA program at the University of Tennessee, Knoxville, and the undergraduate business program at the University of Oklahoma, Norman.

The **Basics**

Introduction

We, as individuals within our society, harbor many complex myths and truths about money. We view money through the lens of our experiences, or lack thereof, as well as a result of impressions from Wall Street, the media, friends and our families. We also tend to shy away from talking about our finances in a truly personal way, often feeling embarrassed or uncomfortable with sharing where we are in our lives or what we believe to be true. This is unfortunate. We need knowledge to make the best decisions for our lives.

"Plan as if you are going to live forever and live as if you are going to die today."

—R. NELSON NASH

In this book, I am going to talk about money. Whether you are working with a financial advisor/representative or managing your own money, I believe it's important to obtain a comprehensive financial education.

Many people spend a lifetime worrying about their money. They worry about having enough for today and tomorrow. They are concerned about being able to afford to send their kids to college while also having enough money for retirement. They think about how they will support their parents in retirement. Many people are anxious about what funds they will access if they end up unemployed or disabled. People also fear losing their money through poor investment choices. It doesn't have to be this way. There is an alternative financial strategy that can remove the weight of our anxiety and fear of loss.

My main mission for this book is to introduce you to a powerful but misunderstood and underused financial tool, whole life insurance. I want to get you to think about a life long financial strategy using participating permanent whole life insurance. By reading this book, understanding and applying its strategies, you will set yourself on a path to achieve financial stability and freedom.

This book seeks to stretch your comfort zone by challenging the common beliefs and attitudes you have learned and adopted about money. I believe you deserve to live your life with the best possible financial strategy not the latest financial product.

For the purpose of organization, I have structured this book into six chapters.

The Basics, reviews a couple of important basic financial concepts. This section of the book also reviews some of the assumptions underlying our standard financial knowledge that we've come to accept as fact and challenges some of this basic knowledge using a few examples.

Life Insurance, introduces the world of life insurance and the concept of using participating whole life insurance as a financial tool.

A Lifetime Financial Strategy builds upon the educational foundation provided in *Chapters 1* and *2*. *Chapter 3* discusses how the participating whole life insurance policy can be used both as a powerful savings vehicle and a lifetime financial strategy.

Case Studies, consists of a series of evolving case studies that walk you through the power of participating whole life insurance using a child's insurance policy. Each section in *Chapter 4* illustrates how to use the participating whole life insurance contract to finance a car, fund a college education, a wedding, etc. In working through real-life applications using participating whole life insurance you will begin to fully grasp the power of this financial strategy.

Wrapping It All Up, summarizes key concepts.

What's Next? provides some general guidance as to how to take the next steps to further explore participating whole life insurance as a financial strategy with respect to your personal situation.

So let's get started!

The Status Quo

We are constantly being bombarded with all kinds of financial advice, beliefs, and values. Just look at the personal finance section of any library or bookstore. Witness the gurus, talk shows, and discussions about money on television. Look at all the articles and differences of opinion.

As a parent, grandparent, aunt, or uncle, you have most likely considered many different options on how to leave a legacy to your

Table 1	Sample List of Key Financial Products

Focus on Security

Cash
Financial Institution Accounts (savings and checking)
Money Market Accounts
Certificates of Deposit (CDs)
Bonds

- U.S. Treasury Obligations
  - Treasury Bill (T-Bill)
  - Treasury Notes
  - Treasury Bonds
  - Treasury Inflation Protected Securities (TIPS)
- Agency Bonds
- Municipal Bonds
- Corporate Bonds

Fixed Annuity
Preferred Stock
Term Insurance

Focus on Growth

Common Stocks
Mutual Funds
Variable Annuity
Universal Life Insurance Products
Exchange-Traded Funds
Real Estate

Focus on Protection and Growth

Participating Permanent Whole Life Insurance

loved ones or to charities. In addition, you've probably thought more than once about how you'll provide a secure and opportunity-rich future for *yourself* while providing for others. You want to be able to transfer the wealth from one generation to another and provide for the children in your family in a way that teaches responsibility and sound financial stewardship.

There are a lot of places to put money, a veritable buffet of financial choices. I've provided a sample list of some of the financial products and strategies available to us in Table 1. Certainly any solid lifetime financial strategy will employ a number of these financial products. The challenge is to think about each product, explore its purpose and to fully understand how that particular financial product functions. In my opinion, a financial tool or product cannot be labeled as *bad*. Rather, it's important to remember that each of the financial products you may come across was designed to meet a specific need or set of needs with a target goal or purpose in mind.

Each of the financial tools or products you use also comes with a certain set of characteristics related to its risk, rate of return, tax liability, liquidity, and predictability. For example, depositing your money in a savings account at your local bank has a very low risk. While your financial security (or safety) with this type of financial product is high, your rate of return is low. You also pay tax to the United States Government (also possibly state and local taxes) on the interest from the money in your savings account, yet you have high liquidity (the ability to turn your money into cash) and predictability of results.

As this simple savings account example illustrates, there are strengths and weaknesses with each financial product you select. The key is to realize this and plan accordingly. Any financial plan you are going to be able to live with and follow for a lifetime *must*

- be aligned with your values and beliefs about money.

- be based on a comprehensive understanding of the reality of your current *total* financial situation.

- consider your risk tolerance.

- consider the tax implications of your strategy, current and future.

- systematically address how to build wealth while also taking into account lifetime curve balls and unexpected events.

I want to clearly acknowledge that there's absolutely nothing wrong with investing in real estate, bonds, mutual funds, exchange traded funds (ETFs), company stock, or any of the other financial products listed in Table 1. In fact, diversification of risk and careful allocation of your assets is an appropriate strategy to manage your money and your wealth over your lifetime.

However, in today's world, I think we rely too heavily on the stock market. Mutual funds and other investments in your 401(k) should be one aspect of your financial plan, but they should not comprise your total financial plan. We are going to take a closer look at mutual funds and some of the assumptions that we have accepted as fact about this financial product. But first, I want to review some basic commonly confused financial concepts: saving versus investing and financial risk.

Saving versus Investing—There Is a Difference

"A lack of savings discipline handicaps more people than does poor investment returns."

—Donald L. Blanton

Over the years the terms "saving" and "investing" have been combined and used together to describe a variety of financial products. Through common and inaccurate usage, these concepts have overlapped and become fused. We use the terms interchangeably as though they mean the same thing. But they don't. Saving and investing are two very distinct concepts. Your *savings* consist of money that you don't want to lose; whereas, money you *invest* is money that is subject to the risk of loss.

Think back to when you were a kid saving for your first bicycle. Did you give the money that you had saved up to buy your bike to your buddy who told you he could double it in a month or a year but that he might also lose some or all of it? No! You put it in your piggy bank or you let your parents hold on to it and keep track of it. In short, you kept your money someplace where it would be safe from the risk of loss, where you could add to it and eventually you would be able access the full amount.

Any money that you designate as savings should be in a financial vehicle with low risk, where you can access the money, with no fear of loss of the principal. *To be clear: when you have money in the stock market, no matter what it is called, it is an* **investment**, *subject to loss.* Money in a mutual fund or in the stock market may grow and accumulate but this money is always at risk for loss. Saving is really only accomplished in a financial vehicle in which *your money cannot be lost.*

For a solid financial strategy, there should be two groups of money. There should be money that is saved and not subject to risk of loss, and there should be another group of money that is invested.

A proper financial strategy will have these two components clearly distinguished. We need to truly understand that the invested money has the potential for greater growth but also has a greater risk of loss.

To give you an example of how we commonly confuse our thinking with regard to saving and investing, let's look at how we talk about our 401(k). I often have clients tell me that they are saving for retirement in their 401(k). But what are the typical financial products in a 401(k)? Mutual funds. Mutual funds are an *investment product*, **not** a *savings product*, because they expose your money to the risk of loss in the stock market. And loss is just what many people experienced in the last two years (2008 and 2009) with respect to their 401(k) account.

A lot of retirement "savings" accounts are really retirement "investment" accounts. By confusing and blending the fundamental concepts of saving and investing, we confuse the risk associated with our money. By not being clear about whether our money is in a saving or investment product, we can end up believing that our money is less exposed to risk that it really is.

Even the health care accounts are not immune from the confusion between investing and saving. I'll use an example from my own portfolio. I have an opportunity for asset allocation in my Health Savings Account which is held with a major U.S. bank. The bank offers me a choice of six accounts in which to place my Health Savings Account money. Remember, this is supposed to be a Health Savings Account, not a Health Investment Account. However, four of the six choices my bank offers are mutual funds which is an investment vehicle, subject to the risk of loss, and not a savings product. This is a prime example as to why we as consumers get confused between savings and investments.

In recent years I have also witnessed the downgrading of saving as a financial strategy. In our current financial climate we focus on the excitement and possibility of greater returns that the stock market investments may yield. Certainly, in the stock market, it is possible to make larger gains than with a savings product. However, we neglect to think about the impact that the potential loss of our money will have on us, our family and our future.

I'm not suggesting that we give up on the stock market, only that we become more aware of the risks and vicious cycles that chasing returns can be. We put money into the stock market and the stock or mutual fund value drops. We're encouraged to stay in the market because it will "come back" so we continue to buy more stocks, change mutual funds, change advisors, all the while telling ourselves that if we can get that twenty-five percent return, we'll get back the value of our original investment and then some. We tell ourselves (as does everyone else) that, over time, we'll come out ahead. Sometimes we do. But many times we don't. Why? Because we do not understand how much sustained growth it takes to recover our original lost principal. We have also not truly looked at the eroding effect of inflation, taxes and fees on our money.

I'll be working through some basic financial examples so you can better understand the impact of losing a portion of your original principal a little further on. However, what I'd like to propose right now is that we temper our desire to get greater returns in the stock market and rediscover the fundamental value of saving. We have been dazzled by the possibility of greater returns in the stock market while minimizing the risk of loss associated with this potential growth. What we have forgotten is the power of compound interest.

Let's take a quick look at compound interest. Figure 1 illustrates the simple, effective power of compound interest. The graph illustrates the savings potential, starting at different ages (ten, thirty, forty, and fifty) and saving $10,000 per year with 5% interest on this money. Even starting a savings program such as this one at age forty, the power of compound interest means that you could save almost a half a million dollars ($536,691) by age sixty-five and just over one million dollars by age seventy-five. It's not glamorous. It's not exciting. But it is steady, predictable and sustainable growth over your lifetime.

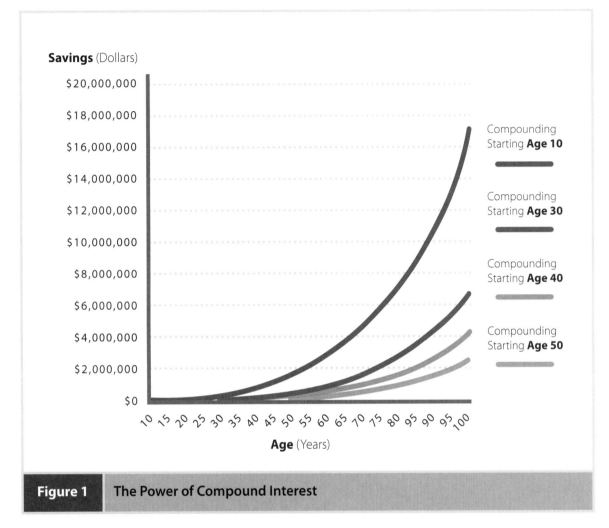

| Figure 1 | The Power of Compound Interest |

Combined with other appropriate financial approaches, saving can form a powerful cornerstone of a lifelong financial strategy.

Another way to look at the difference between savings and investing is to review the definition provided by the Securities and Exchange Commission (SEC). The SEC states:

"Your 'savings' are usually put into the safest places or products that allow you access to your money at any time. Examples

include savings accounts, checking accounts, and certificates of deposit. At some banks and savings and loan associations, your deposits may be insured by the Federal Deposit Insurance Corporation (FDIC). But there is a tradeoff for the security and ready availability of these savings methods: your money is paid a low wage as it works for you."[1]

The SEC also states that "when you 'invest,' you have a greater chance of losing your money than when you 'save.' Unlike FDIC insured deposits, the money you invest in securities, mutual funds, and other similar investments is not federally insured. You could lose your "principal," which is the amount you've invested. That's true even if you purchase your investments through a bank. But when you invest, you also have the opportunity to earn more money than when you save."[2]

Consider a financial strategy that is built on the understanding that saving and investing are not the same thing. You invest for greater growth at the risk of loss, and you save for moderate growth with security and accessibility. You need both sides of the coin for a secure financial future.

| Figure 2 | Two Sides of the Coin |

---

1. "Differences Between Saving and Investing," *U.S. Securities and Exchange Commission,* http://www.sec.gov/rss/ask_investor_ed/saveinvest.htm (accessed September 12, 2009).

2. Ibid.

Understanding Financial Risk

When we talk about financial risk what we are really talking is about the possibility of losing part or all of our original principal. To minimize the risk of loss in the financial marketplace, money (or assets) are often invested using the strategy of diversification. Diversification is an investment management principle which is used to reduce an investor's risk by spreading investments across a variety of different assets, securities and industries. The theory is that you "diversify away" some of your risk without affecting your expected return.[3] Essentially, the concept of diversification is captured by the time-worn phrase "Don't put all your eggs in one basket."

When you diversify, you spread your money among a variety of securities, industries and assets that are referred to as "asset classes." Each asset class is expected to reflect a different financial risk and return and will perform differently in any given market environment.[4] Some asset classes are equities (stocks), fixed-income (bonds), real estate, commodities, cash equivalents (money market instruments) and participating whole life insurance.

As you decide what your personal risk tolerance is, you make a decision as to how to allocate your money among the different asset classes. For example if you are more aggressive in your portfolio and willing to accept higher financial risk of loss, your asset allocation might consist of 75% stocks and 25% bonds. Conversely a more conservative portfolio allocation would comprise 25% stocks and 75% bonds.

Diversification and asset allocation are two core principles used to minimize financial risk. The basic premise is that if one or more investment (or group of investments) does decrease in value, you still

---

3. Arthur J. Keown, *Personal Finance: Turning Money Into Wealth* (Upper Saddle River, New Jersey, Pearson Education, Inc., 2007), page 18.

4. "Asset Class," *Investopedia.com*, http://www.investopedia.com/terms/a/assetclasses.asp (accessed August 13, 2009).

have money in investments that are increasing in value. The thought is that through diversification and asset allocation, you won't suffer too greatly from losses because you have managed the risk with a blended rate of return across all of your assets.

Managing risk through diversification and asset allocation is a good idea; however, what we witnessed in the financial meltdown of 2008 and 2009 is that perhaps risk cannot be quantified with exact certainty. Diversification of our *invested* assets as the sole means of decreasing our exposure to risk may not be enough to protect us from financial loss.

In "The New Rule of Risk Management, Rebuilding the Model," published in *Knowledge@Wharton* on June 24, 2009, three participants at the Oliver Wyman Institute Twelfth Annual Financial Risk Roundtable 2009 were interviewed by the *Knowledge@Wharton* staff.[5] In the interview Richard Herring, a finance professor at Wharton, John Drzik, President and CEO of the Oliver Wyman Group, and Francis Diebold, a Wharton professor of economics and finance statistics, discussed how to build a more informed risk management model.

At this roundtable event, the key question being asked was, Can risk really be measured accurately? In answer to this question, Richard Herring stated that "*the last year [2009] shows that we can't, that there are lots of things we can't quantify very successfully and that we have become overconfident in the things that we could quantify.*"

He went on to say that "*we weren't using enough forward information and unfortunately, this crisis has blame that can be shared across the entire spectrum of participants from regulators to participants in securitizations and even risk managers themselves.*" Francis Diebold concurred stating that "*there's a whole spectrum of risks*" some of which are easy to model and some of which even experts admit they can't predict with great accuracy. For example, as Diebold pointed out, risk can range from

---

5. "The New Role of Risk Management: Rebuilding the Model," *Knowledge@Wharton*, June 24, 2009, http://knowledge.wharton.upenn.edu/article.cfm?articleid=2268 (accessed August 13, 2009).

"*market risk to credit risk to operational risk to legal and reputational risk and things beyond that [. . .] anything ranging from computer system failures to terrorist attacks.*"

Diversification and asset allocation are still important and viable financial concepts. However, what these experts are saying is that while important, diversification of invested assets and asset allocation cannot and do not guarantee your investments protection from all risk. This is what we witnessed in the market meltdown of 2008 and 2009. People had diversified their assets within the stock market but everything decreased in value at the same time, including asset classes such as real estate and bonds.

Points to Review

- This book seeks to stretch your comfort zone by challenging the common beliefs you have learned as well as the attitudes you have adopted about money.

- Each of the financial tools or products you use also comes with a certain set of characteristics related to its risk, rate of return, tax liability, liquidity, and predictability.

- A financial tool or product cannot be labeled as bad. Rather, it's important to remember that each of the financial products you may come across was designed to meet a specific need or set of needs.

- Saving and investing are two very distinct concepts. Your savings consist of money you don't want to lose; whereas money that you are investing is subject to the risk of loss.

- We have been dazzled by the possibility of greater returns in the stock market while minimizing the risk of loss associated with this potential growth. What we have forgotten is the power of compound interest.

- To minimize the risk of loss in the financial marketplace, money (or assets) are generally dealt with through diversification and asset allocation.

- Diversification of risk and asset allocation are important and viable financial concepts. However, while important, diversification of assets and asset allocation cannot and do not guarantee your investments protection from all risk.

Mutual Funds and 401(k)s

Discussing every financial product and vehicle available is outside the scope of this book. However, since investment in mutual funds is the most commonly employed and recommended financial vehicle, I want to explore some of the assumptions about this financial product.

What exactly is a mutual fund? Although we talk or hear about this financial vehicle every day, I think it might be helpful to review the basics.

A mutual fund is an investment vehicle. Money from hundreds or thousands of investors is pooled together for the purpose of investing in securities such as stocks, bonds, money market instruments or other similar assets. Mutual funds are operated by money managers. The responsibility of the money managers is to invest the fund's capital in an attempt to produce capital gains and income for the fund's investors.[6] Each investor in a mutual fund owns shares which represent a portion of the fund. Mutual funds earn dividends on stocks and interest on bonds and then

"I suppose if I were to give advice it would be to keep out of Wall Street."

—John D. Rockefeller

---

6. "Mutual Fund," *Investopedia.com*, http://www.investopedia.com/terms/m/mutualfund.asp (accessed August 13, 2009).

pay out this income to fund owners as distributions or the investor may choose to reinvest their dividends back into the mutual fund.

When you contribute money to a fund, you get a stake in all of its investments. This is significant since some funds allow you to begin investing with as little as twenty-five dollars. Consequently, you can attain a diversified portfolio for much less money than you could by buying individual stocks and bonds. Plus, you don't have to worry about keeping track of dozens of holdings. That's the money manager's job.

There are more than 21,000 different mutual funds.[7] In fact, there are more mutual funds than there are stocks.[8] This means that you have a huge variety of mutual funds from which to choose.

The money you invest can be grouped into two categories:

- Qualified Plans

- Nonqualified Plans

A *Qualified Plan* is an investment vehicle that qualifies for special tax treatment under the Internal Revenue Code. There are many different types of qualified plans, but most fall into two categories:

1. Defined Benefit Plan

2. Defined Contribution Plan

A *Defined Benefit Plan* (e.g., a traditional pension plan) is funded by employer/employee contributions and provides you with a specified level of retirement benefits.

---

7. Morningstar Principia Database, (accessed August 12, 2009).

8. "Mutual Fund," *Economic Expert*, http://www.economicexpert.com/a/Mutual:funds.html (accessed August 12, 2009).

A *Defined Contribution Plan* (e.g., a profit-sharing, 403(b) or 401(k) plan) is funded by the employer and/or employee contributions. The benefits you receive from this type of plan plan depend on investment performance.[9]

The annual contribution limits and other rules vary among specific types of plans. However, most qualified plans share certain key features, including the following:

- Pre-tax contributions: Contributions to a qualified plan (both employer and employee) up to certain limits are made on a pre-tax basis. You don't pay income tax on the amounts contributed until you withdraw money from the plan.

- Tax-deferred growth: Capital gains and investment earnings (e.g., dividends and interest) on all contributions grow tax deferred. Alternatively, losses in these plans are not tax deductible.

- Deferred tax calculation: You don't pay income tax on those capital gains or investment earnings until you withdraw these gains or earnings from the plan. Once withdrawn from the plan, capital gains and investment earning are then taxed at ordinary income tax rates.

- Creditor protection: In most cases, your creditors cannot access your qualified retirement plan funds to satisfy your debts until you take distributions. However, once you have taken a distribution, this money is then potentially accessible to creditors.

---

9. "What does the term 'qualified plan' mean?," *360 Financial Literacy*, http://www.360financialliteracy.org/Women/Planning+For+Your+Future/FAQs/ What+does+the+term +qualified+plan+mean.htm (accessed August 12, 2009).

Qualified Plans include the 403(b) and 401(k) Plan, Traditional Individual Retirement Plan (IRA), Keogh Plan, Simplified Employee Pension Plan (SEP-IRA), Roth IRA, Savings Incentive Match Plan for Employees (SIMPLE), and Stretch IRA. Other qualified plans not related to retirement include the Health Savings Account (HSA) and 529 College Saving Plans.

Nonqualified Plans are retirement plans that do not meet the qualifications for special tax treatment as set forth in the Internal Revenue Code. Investment income from such a plan is treated by the Internal Revenue Service (IRS) as ordinary taxable income, dividend income or a capital gain and is taxed in the year earned.

Investors may also hold mutual funds outside a retirement plan. Since these are not considered "qualified funds," the gains, interest and dividends are fully taxable and realized losses are deductible if certain requirements are met.

Assumptions and Limitations of Mutual Funds in Qualified Plans

"The return of your money is more important than the return on your money."

—WILL ROGERS

Since most of us own a 401(k) or some other type of qualified retirement plan listed above, let's spend a little time looking at these plans. In almost every article about personal finances, the same advice is repeated to us; put the maximum allowable amount of money into a qualified plan. Again, having some funds in this type of account is prudent, but to use this vehicle as the foundation of your financial strategy can have some serious limitations, as we've observed recently with the 2008–2009 stock market fluctuations and downturn in the economy.

Let's take a closer look at some of the assumptions and risks with mutual funds in qualified plans that don't seem to get discussed much.

First, let's list the statements we've all come to know regarding 401(k)s and other qualified plans. These assumptions are often stated as if they are fact. . . . They're not.

Common Qualified Plan *assumptions* regarding your *tax situation:*

- Tax savings and tax deferral are always desirable objectives.

- By taking advantage of a qualified plan, you are saving yourself a lot of money in two ways. First, by taking the tax deduction associated with the qualified plan you reduce your taxable income and, consequently, the amount of income tax you pay. Second, by placing your money in a qualified plan, you defer the tax calculation on this money until your retirement.

- You will be in a lower tax bracket when you retire, so you will pay less tax when you withdraw your money.

Common Qualified Plan *assumptions* regarding the *growth of your investment:*

- Your mutual fund value will increase at a linear rate of 8% (approximate long-term stock market average growth rate) and your investment will increase if you stay invested in the stock market long enough.

- When you are ready to retire, you will have more money in the mutual funds within your qualified plan than you do now.

Tax Assumptions

OK, let's take a closer look at the assumption regarding taxes and qualified retirement plans. First, we always assume that tax savings and deferral are the best fit for your overall financial plan. When we're filling out our income tax return, this does seem especially poignant and true. However, think about it. For tax deferral to be a good plan, you're assuming that tax rates won't increase. You don't know what the tax calculation on your money will be when you are going to withdraw funds from your qualified plan. You *hope* that any future tax increase won't be more than the tax rates today. A recent article in *Time Magazine* by Justin Fox entitled "A Fun-Free Recovery" (June 29, 2009) stated, *". . . there's just no way to square the cost of current recession-fighting efforts, future Medicare commitments and the various goals of the Obama Administration with the current level of taxation. Taxes are going to have to go up and raising rates on just the very richest won't be enough."* [10]

Also, we hear the statement, "You're in a higher tax bracket now, so you defer paying the tax today for some time in the future." The rationale goes like this: when you pull your money out at retirement, then you'll be in a lower tax bracket and, therefore, pay less tax. But how are tax brackets calculated? By income! Do you really want to retire with a significantly lower income than you have now? Isn't this the worst-case scenario? Ideally I would think you would like to have at least as much annual income as you have now. When I think about my retirement, I don't want to worry about having enough money to pay my monthly bills or future medical expenses. Instead, I want to travel, enjoy my hobbies, and live the kind of life I dreamed of when retired.

Finally, I believe the most misunderstood tax issue is the concept of *tax deferral,* or delaying paying tax on your money until you take

10. Justin Fox, "A Fun-Free Recovery," *Time Magazine*, June 29, 2009.

it out of your qualified plan. When you defer income tax within the structure of a qualified plan, you end up paying tax on the "harvest," not the "seed."

Let's look at an example of tax deferral using some simple math.

Assume you put $100 in your 401(k) today. Let's say that you are in a 30% tax bracket, so you delay paying $30 of tax on this money. Over the long-term, this $100 investment sits inside your 401(k) and grows to $1,000. Now when you take it out, instead of paying $30 (30% of $100) in tax, you're paying $300 (30% of $1,000). You deferred paying the $30 tax on the "seed" and now you are paying $300 on the "harvest."

In this scenario, considering you've made $700 on your investment inside your 401(k), you might say, "Hey, I'll pay a little more tax." But what if you had lost money inside this 401(k)? You delayed paying tax initially, but now when you need all your money, you're going to pay the current ordinary income tax rate on what little may be left.

Let's take a closer look at a tax deferment example and the impact of market fluctuations, capital losses and taxes assuming that you start with $500,000 in your qualified plan.

If you have $500,000 in your qualified plan and the market drops 40% as it did during 2008 to 2009, then your $500,000 is now reduced by $200,000. You're left with a qualified plan value of $300,000. Say you now need to access this money to pay your mortgage, college tuition for your child(ren) and other normal living expenses. Under current IRS rules (as of 2009), you need to be at least age fifty-nine and one-half before you can withdraw money within your qualified plan without a 10% penalty. Assuming you're older than fifty-nine and one-half (and in a 30% tax bracket) then you will pay a 30% ordinary income tax rate on the money you withdraw from your plan. (Remember, if you're younger than fifty-nine and one-half, you need to add an additional 10% penalty tax to these numbers).

"Insanity is doing the same thing over and over again and expecting different results."

—ALBERT EINSTEIN
(attributed)

Example 1	**Impact of Market Fluctuations, Capital Losses and Taxes**

Qualified Plan Value:	$ 500,000
40% Stock Market Drop	$(200,000)
Resulting Qualified Plan Value	$ 300,000
Taxes (30%) on $300,000	$ (90,000)
	$ 210,000

Percentage Remaining: $\dfrac{\$\,210{,}000}{\$\,500{,}000} = 42\%$

As a result of market fluctuations, capital loss and taxes; you now have 42% of your qualified plan value to live on.

OK, assuming you're older than fifty-nine and one-half, if you take $300,000 out of your plan, then you will pay $90,000 in taxes (30% of 300,000). After it's all said and done, you will be left with $210,000. You lost 58% of your money due to the stock market drop and taxes. Your remaining $210,000 is 42% of the money you originally had in your qualified plan. This is also the very real effect of stock market fluctuation, capital loss, taxes and out of sync timing between your life needs and the stock market. I've summarized the math in Example 1.

Market Assumptions

This leads us to the next assumption with mutual funds in qualified plans: if you just stay in the stock market long enough, the stock market will go up and so will your investment.

I have a couple of comments about this.

First, since when are our lives and financial needs and wants perfectly correlated to the stock market? Although the overall market trend of the stock market has been one of growth, what if you need retirement income during one of the numerous downturns in the market? It's convenient and easy to say, "Stay in the stock market." But when confronted by a life changing event such as retirement, college, health concerns, divorce, or job loss, we may need to access our money.

I encourage you to look at the only statistic of any importance: the money in your investment and savings accounts.

Over the past several decades, we have witnessed that the downturns are significant compared to the upturns. In his article in *The Wall Street Journal* (July 11, 2009), Jason Zweig noted that "*As of June 30, U.S. stocks have underperformed long-term Treasury bonds for the past five, ten, fifteen, twenty and twenty-five years.*"[11]

Alexandra Twin of CNNMoney.com observed in her March 2009 online article that, "*Since closing at its all-time high of 14,164.53 on Oct. 9, 2007, the Dow has lost nearly 54%. The S&P 500, which also hit its high of 1565.15 on Oct. 9 has lost around 57%.*"[12]

It's not pretty out there, as you well know. But rather than trying to continue to prove my point with all kinds of statistics, I encourage

---

11. Jason Zweig, "The Intelligent Investor: Does Stock Market Data Really Go Back 200 Years?" *The Wall Street Journal*, July 11, 2009.

12. Alexandra Twin, "For Dow, Another 12-year Low," *CNNMoney.com*, March 9, 2009, http://money.cnn.com/2009/03/09/markets/markets_newyork/index.htm (accessed August 12, 2009).

you to look at the only statistic of any importance: the money in your investment and savings accounts.

How much money do you have right now? Over the years, how much money have you put in your 401(k), your brokerage account at your financial advisor's company, and/or any other place where you have invested money in the stock market? Think about how much of your income you have put into these various places and how much money you have now. This is *the* most important statistic.

Do you have more money in your account this year than last year and how much is at risk?

In speaking with clients from all over the country, many tell me that they have less money now than they had when they started their investments. But they are still hearing that if they hang on long enough in the stock market, they will come out ahead. Oh, and by the way, they are getting a *great* average rate of return. The critical problem is that some of these folks are ready to retire now! They don't have another ten years to wait hoping that the stock market will improve and taxes don't increase.

Remember, the most important statistic is the account balance of your statements that you open every month, quarter, or year. Do you have more money in your account than last year? And perhaps the most important questions are; "How much of your investment is at risk?" and, "Can you afford to lose your money if the stock market tumbles again or doesn't rise as fast as hoped or predicted?"

"It can be very easy to drift off into a sea of misinformation and drown in the sole pursuit of a magic product."

—Donald L. Blanton

As of March 9, 2009, the stock market was down approximately 54% from a high in October 2007.[13] In round numbers, if you originally had $10,000, and you lost 50% in the stock market, your remaining balance is now $5,000. To get back to the amount you started with, you're going to need to double your

---

13. Ibid.

money, which means getting a 100% return. It takes a lot more time and effort to gain 100% than to lose 50%.

As you can see from Table 2, protecting against a capital loss is of critical importance since the greater your loss, the harder it is just to get back to your original starting point. This becomes painfully evident when you combine a capital loss with the erosion of your wealth due to taxes, inflation and other factors that drain away your money.

Table 2	Example Effect of Stock Market Drop		
Starting Balance	Percentage Loss	Ending Balance	% Increase Required to Return to Starting Value
$10,000	(25%)	$7,500	33%[1]
$10,000	(40%)	$6,000	66%
$10,000	(50%)	$5,000	100%

1. Example Calculation: $7,500 x 1.333 = $9,997.50

Due to the poor performance of the stock market in the past decade, retirement accounts have lost from $2 trillion to $4 trillion as stocks have tumbled nearly 50% from their peak in 2007.[14] Retired people or folks ready to retire who followed traditional financial advice are being told to take on part-time jobs, move out of their communities away from their children and grandchildren into cheaper neighborhoods, and withdraw less from their dwindling market-based investments.

Remember, historic stock market performance is not a predictor of future performance.

In actuality, we are trying to build a secure financial foundation on money that we are gambling with in the stock market. Our largest traditional financial planning vehicles, such as mutual funds within a 401(k), do not produce predictable outcomes. How can they when the stock market is inherently unpredictable? Mutual funds come with no guarantees of investment growth. Their performance is measured

---

14. "Not So Golden: Employees—and Employers—Feel the Pinch from Shortfalls in Retirement Funding," *Knowledge@Wharton*, April 1, 2009, http://knowledge.wharton.upenn.edu/article.cfm?articleid=2193 (accessed August 12, 2009).

by looking back and calculating the average rate of return on money invested in the fund. We are depending upon the undependable for our long-term financial stability.

The question to ask yourself is, "What will the value of my mutual fund be next week, next year, or in five, ten or twenty years?" The only real answer is: "I don't know." Remember, historic performance is not a predictor of future performance.

Let's close this chapter by examining what an "average rate of return" really means to you and your investments.

In actuality, we are trying to build a secure financial foundation on money that we are gambling with in the stock market.

Average Rate of Return is not the same as Compound Interest

Terminology can be confusing. With respect to your investments, this lack of clarity can cost you dearly. One thing you can always trust, however, is your own understanding of some financial fundamentals and some basic math.

When we talk about our money, it's helpful to follow the numbers. Financial reports for our mutual funds talk about "market averages" and report the "average rate of return" to summarize their mutual fund performance. To better explain the concept of average rate of return and what this means to your investment, I'm going to walk you through a simple example.

Let's say you have $10,000 and you give it to me to invest in a mutual fund, which I've told you should earn an average rate of return of 25% over four years based upon its past performance.

In the first year the money goes up 100%. During the second year, unfortunately, the money goes down by 50%. Ouch! It's not looking good, but hang in there; it will come back. In the third year, it goes up 100%. But in the fourth year, it goes down 50% again.

"All truths are easy to understand once they are discovered; the point is to discover them."

—Galileo Galilei

Table 3	Average Rate of Return
Year	Market
1	+100%
2	−50%
3	+100%
4	−50%
Average Rate of Return = 25%	

So let's do the math here: 100% minus 50% plus 100% minus 50% = 100% divided by 4 (years) gives you an average rate of return of 25%. I've illustrated this market fluctuation in Table 3.

I told you that I would work hard to get you an average annual rate of return of 25%, and here it is. I have fulfilled my promise to you. However, here's the problem: When we think of a 25% average rate of return over four years, most people think of a *linear progression* of 25% compounded each and every year. This means, that contrary to reality, in our minds we calculate our return as: $10,000 × 1.25 × 1.25 × 1.25 × 1.25 = $24,414. This is not correct. Average rate of return is *not* the same concept as compound interest.

Using the same example as above, let's see what your money is potentially doing while it's making an average rate of return of 25%.

You put in $10,000. The first year it goes up 100%, so you have $20,000. It goes down 50% the second year, so you have $10,000. In the third year, it goes up 100%, so you are back up to $20,000. During the fourth year, it goes down 50%, and you are back down to $10,000, the amount you started with as I've shown in Table 4.

So even though you received an average rate of return of 25% on your money over four years, note that *your investment is not 25% larger year by year over the past four years.* The sad truth is that at the end of this four-year period, you will likely have

Table 4	Following Your Money Through an Average Rate of Return of 25%		
Year	Market	Starting Balance	Ending Balance
1	+100%	$10,000	$20,000
2	−50%	$20,000	$10,000
3	+100%	$10,000	$20,000
4	−50%	$20,000	$10,000
Average Rate of Return = 25%			

less than when you started with because along the way there have been sales charges, fees, and other expenses (which, to keep things straightforward, I have conveniently not accounted for in the above example).

The point is that the average rate of return is not as important to you as the amount of money in your account. What do you care if your fund boasts a 10%, 15%, or 25% rate of return if your cash balance is not increasing? *Follow your cash and not the average rate of return.*

Points to Review

- When you place money in a qualified plan, you defer the tax and you also defer the tax calculation. It does not necessarily mean you will pay less tax.

- *The average rate of return is not equal to compound interest.* Remember that an average rate of return of 25% does not necessarily mean that you are growing your wealth at this rate. It also does not guarantee that you will not lose money.

- The most important statistic is the account balance of your statements that you open every month, quarter, or year. Do you have more money in your account than last year? Perhaps the most important questions are; "How much is at risk? and "Can you afford to lose your money if the stock market tumbles again or doesn't rise as fast as predicted?"

- Staying in the stock market "long enough" does not guarantee an increase in your investment account.

- The stock market highs don't always coincide with when you need or want your money.

- Mutual fund historic performance is not a predictor of future performance.

Social Security and Planning for Retirement

Many books still recommend a retirement planning approach referred to as "The Three Legged Stool." The basic premise of this strategy is that we need to rely on three components for our financial security in retirement: 1) company pension plans (sometimes called defined benefit plans), 2) Social Security, and 3) personal savings. I believe this strategy is woefully out of date.

First, we live in an era that has witnessed a dramatic decrease in company pension plans. Many companies have switched to the 401(k) model making it the employee's responsibility to invest and save for retirement. The company may contribute matching funds to the 401(k), but as we have seen in 2008 and 2009, many companies have opted out of matching funds. Companies have also entered bankruptcy and transferred their company pension obligations to the Pension Benefit Guaranty Corporation (PBGC). (This is a federal agency created by the Employee Retirement Income Security Act of 1974 (ERISA) to protect pension benefits in private-sector traditional pension plans known as defined benefit plans).[15]

Second, Social Security is quickly losing its ability to pay its obligations. In 1935, when Social Security was created, the official pension age was sixty-five, three years beyond the lifespan of the typical American. In fact, "Social Security was designed to be a brief sunset to life for a few hearty souls."[16]

But now our life expectancy is much longer. Life insurance tables have been revised and now extend to age 121. Social Security was never intended for the general population to live on in retirement for ten, twenty or more years.

Will Social Security be a viable source of retirement revenue for you and me? I don't know. However, in response to this question, I can offer a quote directly from my own social security statement dated October 31, 2009. It's written by Michael J. Astrue, the Social Security Commissioner.

---

15. "Your Guaranteed Pension," *Pension Benefit Guaranty Corporation*, http://www.pbgc.gov/ workers-retirees/benefits-information/content/page14090.html (accessed August 10, 2009).

16. "Ageing in the Rich World. The End of Retirement," *The Economist,* June 25, 2009.

"Social Security is a compact between generations. For decades, America had kept the promise of security for its workers and their families. Now, however, the Social Security system is facing serious financial problems, and action is needed soon to make sure the system will be sound when today's younger workers are ready for retirement.

In 2016 we will begin paying more in benefits than we collect in taxes. Without changes, by 2037 the Social Security Trust Fund will be exhausted* and there will be enough money to pay only about 76 cents for each dollar of scheduled benefits. We need to resolve these issues soon to make sure Social Security continues to provide a foundation of protection for future generations.

*These estimates are based on the intermediate assumptions from Social Security Trustees' Annual Report to Congress."[17]

I believe this statement by the Social Security Commissioner is a call to action for each of us to take responsibility and be accountable for our own financial future. As we've discussed so far, two of the three legs of the financial stool (company pension plans and Social Security) are outdated and failing.

The third leg of the stool is saving. As Americans tapped into easy lines of credit during the housing boom in the late 1990's through 2007, the personal saving rate during this time dipped below zero. In May 2009, the personal saving rate in the U.S. rose to 6.9%.[18] This saving rate was the highest since December 1993. Clearly, although we may be saving more, our savings alone will not be enough to sustain us through our retirement if the majority of our "retirement money" is subject to loss in the stock market.

---

17. Michael J. Astrue, "Your Social Security Statement, What Social Security Means To You," *Social Security Administration*, October 31, 2009.

18. "National Economic Accounts," *U.S. Department of Commerce, Bureau of Economic Analysis*, http://www.bea.gov/newsreleases/national/pi/pinewsrelease.htm (accessed August 5, 2009).

"The only source of financial security you can control and count on is your own money!"

—Donald L. Blanton

By all statistics, tumultuous times are ahead. Remember, *we* supply money to the government via taxes. Currently, our nation is carrying almost $12 trillion in debt.[19] Since the estimated population of the U.S. is 306,735,195, each citizen's share of this debt is currently approximately $39,002.

The new way to plan for the future is to be accountable and responsible for your own money rather than relying on employer and government programs to remain solvent and relevant in the face of a changing and challenging economy.

Points to Review

- We live in an era that has witnessed a dramatic decrease in employee pension plans. Many companies have switched to the 401(k) model making it our responsibility to invest and save for retirement.

- Social Security is quickly losing its ability to pay its obligations.

- Although we may be saving more, our traditional method of saving alone will not be enough to sustain us through our retirement.

- The traditional "Three Legged Stool" approach to retirement planning (i.e., relying on a company pension or defined benefit plan, Social Security and personal savings) is outdated.

---

19. As of October 20, 2009, the national debt was $11,963,480,017,952. Source: Monthly Statement of the Public Debt (MSPD) and Downloadable Files, *Treasury Direct*, http://www.treasurydirect.gov/govt/reports/pd/mspd/mspd.htm (accessed October 20, 2009).

Another Way to Plan for the Future

Any financial plan that is based upon a hoped-for return in the stock market (or in any market, for that matter) is *not* a plan, it's a wish. An effective and appropriately crafted lifetime financial strategy will work in strong or weak economic times.

We've now explored some basic financial concepts and discussed the assumptions and limitations of our most popular investment vehicle, mutual funds in our qualified plans. We've also touched on the key limitations by relying on any company pension or the government to help fund our retirement.

In *Chapters 2* through *4* of this book, I want to introduce you to the concept of using a participating permanent whole life insurance contract as a financial tool. What this means is that you can learn how to use your whole life insurance policy to buy a car, pay for college, a wedding, supplement your retirement and cover your lifetime financial needs and wants. As I mentioned at the start of this chapter, it's a concept and practice that has been around for a very long time. It's a financial staple of the wealthy and is currently standard business practice for executives, corporations and banks.

A properly designed participating whole life policy can function as a simple and powerful financial tool for operating a secure savings plan as part of a lifetime financial strategy. It can be used as a stand-alone strategy or in combination with other investment vehicles and approaches.

Let's start by first taking a closer look at what life insurance is really all about.

Life **Insurance**

Introduction to Life Insurance

Life insurance has been available for purchase in the United States since the mid-1700's. Life insurance protects human life value by creating an estate. Effectively, this means that when the person who is covered by the insurance (referred to as "the insured") dies, a definite sum of money (called a "death benefit") is paid to the beneficiary. Among many uses, this money can be used to meet current obligations of the survivors such as funeral costs, the mortgage and medical bills, to pay for future expenses (e.g., college, weddings, etc.), and to serve as continuing income for the beneficiary.

There are two types of life insurance, *permanent* and *term*.

Permanent insurance is intended to remain in force for the insured's entire life. *Term* life insurance provides insurance for a stated time period. Term insurance can be purchased to cover different time spans such as ten, twenty, and thirty-year periods.

Both term and permanent life insurance provide a death benefit. However, unlike term, permanent life insurance can also provide what are referred to as "living benefits." Living benefits provide a financial resource for you to use and enjoy *during your lifetime*. For example, with permanent life insurance it's possible to take policy loans, use the life insurance policy for collateral on bank loans, or use the policy for retirement income, cash withdrawals, and more. Living benefits are provided by the accumulation of cash value *and* the death benefit inside the permanent life insurance policy.

There are many different types of life insurance products on the market today. Each insurance company has their own life insurance product line. Some insurance products, such as Universal Life Insurance, Variable Universal, and Equity Index Universal Life Insurance, are insurance products that *share* security products. That is, these products have characteristics of a whole life policy in combination with being associated with the stock market. Since these life insurance products are dependent on interest rates or the stock market they inherently harbor more risk than insurance policies that do not have these characteristics.

In this book, I am dealing specifically with the application of the *permanent, participating whole life insurance policy* as a financial tool and strategy. The term *participating* is used to describe any insurance policy that pays a dividend to its policy owners.

Next, let's review some key components of whole life insurance.

Participating Whole Life Insurance

Insurance Company Structure

Insurance companies are organized as either publicly traded or private companies. A publicly traded company is owned by the shareholders and its shares are registered *securities* for sale to the general public, typically through a stock exchange. They are called stock companies.

A mutual company is a private company operating solely for the benefit of its participating life policy owners. Unlike publicly traded stock-based companies, there are no outside stockholders to share in the profits, so the insurance company is not subject to short-term performance demands of the stock market or the need to show quarterly or annual earnings to satisfy shareholder needs. The company is owned by the policy owners.

With respect to the whole life insurance contract, I believe that mutual companies are able to keep more clearly focused on the benefits for their policy owners because of the singularity of their stated mission which is simply to protect the long-term interests of the policy owners.

Mutual Insurance Companies and Banks

There are some important differences between banks and mutual insurance companies worth noting. These points will be important in our later discussion on using insurance as a financial tool.

Banks in the U.S. operate using fractional reserve banking. This is a practice in which commercial banks are required to keep only a fraction of the money deposited with them as reserves. For example, if the reserve requirement is 10%, and you deposit $100 in your bank, your bank will then lend out $90 (keeping $10 for reserve) of your $100 deposit.

The fractional reserve system works because, usually, the total amount of withdrawals is offset by deposits made at the same time. You can also see how a bank is critically dependent upon borrowers making their loan payments regularly and on time. Another critical aspect of the fractional reserve system is consumer confidence. When people's confidence in the banking system is shaken, bank runs can happen.

"Mutually owned rivals [of stock companies] haven't asked for a dime [of the $700 billion Wall Street bailout money]. Their statutory surpluses (the regulatory counterpart to book value) have held steady or even increased."

—"Mutual Respect,"
Forbes, December 22, 2008

This occurs when many people withdraw their money at the same time.

Compare this system with the insurance world. Insurers *maintain reserves* for the payment of losses or claims and expenses. Reserves are funds created for the purpose of paying anticipated claims under insurance policies. In other words, unlike banks, insurance companies are required by law to maintain reserves set aside to pay future claims.

It's interesting to note that mutual life insurance companies are among the largest and most consistently profitable financial institutions. In fact, there are many American life insurance companies in business today which trace their roots to the early part of the 19th century. During the past 150 years, we have witnessed a cycle of boom and bust for the banking industry; but the insurance industry has maintained a tradition of paying its claims through economic good and bad times. This legacy continues today. This is why financial professionals are able to recommend participating whole life among other insurance industry products as safe and predictable investments.

The entire capitalist economic structure is built on the structural underpinnings of the insurance industry. Insurance is the foundation of our system. This is especially observable in the lending and banking industry, because lenders rely on insurance companies to insure the collateral which backs the loan agreement. When a consumer finances a car, a boat, a home, an apartment complex or other asset, the bank requires insurance. Why? If that asset is lost, damaged or destroyed, the lending institution is able to rely on the ability of the insurance company to replace or pay up to the policy limits for the collateral.

Insurance companies operate within a unique regulatory structure and under specific legal requirements. Due to this oversight, they have avoided many of the ills which seem to plague the banking industry. Insurance executives are aware that they must invest the premiums of their customers prudently, because someday the policy may have to be paid.

To sum up the major difference between banks and mutual insurance companies: banks are leveraged against their deposits while insurance companies are not. This has long-term and long-range implications for the stability of participating whole life contracts as I'll discuss next.

The Whole Life Insurance Contract and its Basic Components

The whole life insurance policy is a private, legal contract between the policy owner, the insured, and the insurance company. You are entering into a defined arrangement with the insurance company and there are very specific contractual elements that protect you.

Participating whole life insurance is contracted to last for the insured's whole (entire) life. The policy owner pays a premium, and these premiums create a growing cash asset, referred to as the "policy's cash value." The policy's cash value is a living benefit and is separate from the death benefit provided by the policy.

Whole life policies have guaranteed cash value and a non-guaranteed dividend. The guaranteed cash value is the amount in the policy if the company were never to pay dividends. How the cash value of your whole life policy is calculated varies depending upon the particular policy and insurance company. However, with all whole life policies, your cash value grows as long as you pay the premiums regularly and on time.

Dividend payments are set annually by the insurance company's board of directors of the mutual company and are not guaranteed (although most mutual insurance companies have paid these dividends continuously for well over 100 years). Insurance companies use different methods to determine dividends although they are often based upon the company's financial results, mortality claims experience and expense control.

Once dividends are paid they become part of the cash value within your policy. Dividends grow tax deferred while in the policy.

The premium is the money you pay the insurance company on a regular, periodic basis in order to obtain a specific amount of insurance. In the case of whole life insurance, "base premium" refers to the basic premium you must pay to keep the policy in force.

In addition to the base premium, you can also purchase paid up additional insurance, commonly referred to as "paid up additions." Paid up additions give you, the policy owner, the option to purchase additional insurance inside your life insurance policy. These paid up additions have cash values, earn additional dividends and increase the death benefit.

The real value of using paid up additions is that you increase the amount of money that you put into your policy. The increase in the amount of money in your policy causes the death benefit and your cash value to compound. By using paid up additions to increase the cash value and death benefit within your policy, you are effectively driving the dividend contribution to almost a multiplier effect with respect to the policy's cash value. Consequently, paid up additions add a tremendous amount of growth potential within the policy. We'll take a closer look at this effect later in *Chapter 4, Case Studies.*

As the policy owner, the cash value in your policy is always yours. The insurance company manages and invests the money and pays policy owners dividends by investing the premiums in conservative investments. However, the policy owners always have first right to their money. You can access the cash value of your policy at any time.

As the policy owner, you can borrow against your policy using the cash value as collateral for the loan from the insurance company. Even when you have a loan outstanding on your policy, your policy receives a dividend. You may repay your loan on any schedule you feel comfortable with, creating *your own* repayment terms. You decide

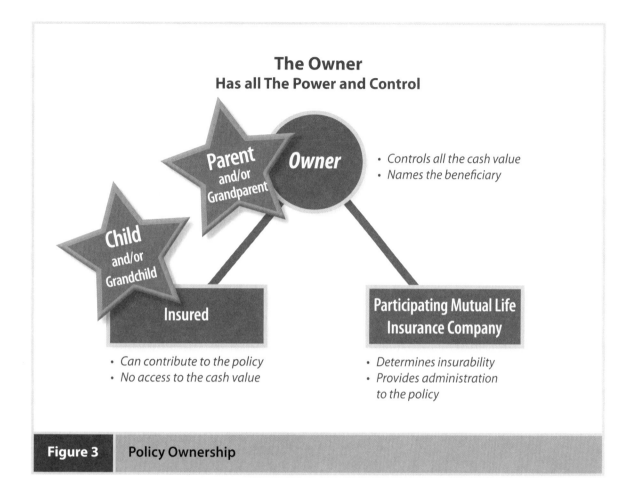

The Owner
Has all The Power and Control

Parent
and/or
Grandparent

Owner

- *Controls all the cash value*
- *Names the beneficiary*

Child
and/or
Grandchild

Insured

- *Can contribute to the policy*
- *No access to the cash value*

Participating Mutual Life Insurance Company

- *Determines insurability*
- *Provides administration to the policy*

Figure 3	**Policy Ownership**

how much to pay on your loan every month. Best of all, the loans you receive are not considered taxable income. If your loan or loan interest is not repaid at your time of death, it is simply subtracted from the death benefit.

There are a few more insurance concepts that are important to introduce and briefly discuss: riders and policy ownership. Riders are additional contractual options that you can have added to your life insurance policy. There is an additional cost to add a rider to your policy. For example, *guaranteed insurability* is a commonly used rider. A guaranteed insurability rider allows you to purchase additional separate whole life insurance policies at specified ages of the insured's life without proof of medical insurability. For example, with this rider in place, the insured could purchase additional life insurance policies even though his/her health had deteriorated.

The *waiver of premium* rider is another common choice among policy owners. This rider guarantees that if the policy owner becomes disabled and is unable to pay the premiums they will continue to be paid by the insurance company. Therefore, with this rider in place, the policy will continue to provide increased cash value, net death benefit and dividends as if the policy owner had not become disabled.

With respect to policy ownership, an important point to make is that it is possible to own an insurance contract on someone else. (Figure 3). In other words, while you can certainly own a whole life policy on yourself, many individuals own one (or several) policies on other people, including their spouse, sibling(s), child(ren), grandchild(ren), niece(s), nephew(s), or business partner(s). A requirement of owning a policy on someone else is that you must have an "insurable interest" in that person. That is, the policy owner must have interest in the continued life of the insured.

Whole Life Policy Design

Not all participating whole life policies are created equal. In fact, there are significant variations in the power and flexibility of the whole life contracts offered by the different mutual insurance companies. A whole life contract that can be used as a financial tool and a lifelong strategy must meet specific design criteria. Your current individual financial status and future requirements are also critical factors in designing a whole life contract that will work effectively for you and your family as a long-term financial tool. It is *absolutely not* the case that "one size fits all."

To recap, the four important design elements and working parts of a participating whole life policy are premiums, cash value, dividends and death benefit. The way that three of these policy components (premium, cash value and death benefit) are specifically designed to work together creates the basic source of power for using whole life as a financial tool. If these three components of a whole life policy are not designed specifically for use as a financial tool, the policy will not perform well in this capacity.

Life Insurance as a Financial Vehicle

Funding a participating whole life contract from a highly rated mutual insurance company is just as easy as contributing to a 401(k), if not easier. You put the money into the whole life policy in the form of premium payments. Your money is not in the stock market and is working for you with minimal risk. There is no need for annual balancing or realigning your asset allocation. You don't have to read financial journals or watch the stock report. Why? Because you aren't worried about what is happening with the Dow or S&P 500. Once your money is inside a properly designed whole life policy, you have access to the cash value without penalty or tax. If you pay your premiums on time, the cash value cannot go down; *it can only go up*.

If you are unable to pay your premiums at any point in time, you can borrow against your policy and then put it right back in as a premium payment. This allows you the flexibility to manage changing life situations such as job loss, health issues or a family emergency.

Essentially, a participating whole life policy is a great financial vehicle in which to save money for the long-term (15 years plus). But there are more concrete and specific benefits to whole life

"Money is a guarantee that we may have what we want in the future. Though we need nothing at the moment, it insures the possibility of satisfying a new desire when it arises."

—Aristotle

than simply depositing cash (in the form of premium payments) in your policy. Let's take a brief look at some of the important living benefits of using whole life insurance as a part of your financial strategy.

Living Benefits of Whole Life Insurance

The list below summarizes the main advantages of using whole life as a financial vehicle. You will notice that these benefits are living benefits, meaning they are providing a financial resource for you to use and enjoy *during your lifetime*. These living benefits are in addition to the legacy provided by the death benefit that will be left to your beneficiaries.

- Liquidity, use, and control of your money

- Access to credit

- Tax-favored environment

- Reduced interest paid to others

- No government involvement

- Insurance for life

- Predictable financial results

- Guaranteed insurability

- Guaranteed cash accumulation

- Creditor proof—protected asset (in certain states)

Now I want to walk you through each one of these benefits and what they mean to you.

Liquidity, Use, and Control of Your Money[1]

In accounting terms, liquidity means that you can convert an asset to cash in less than twelve months. What I mean when I talk about liquidity with respect to your whole life policy is that you can convert your cash value into cash without penalty or tax usually within two weeks. This positions you to take advantage of a financial opportunity or to pay for emergency expenses.

Use means that you have the money available to put to use for any purpose you desire without restrictions.

Control means that you determine the terms, conditions, or repayment terms for the use of *your* money. If you want to change the location of your money, spend it, loan it, or invest it, there are no penalties, no age restrictions and no one to tell you that you can't do what you want to do.

"The ideal investment portfolio is both solid and liquid at the same time."

—Jason Zweig

The unfortunate truth is that most of us do not have liquidity, use, and control of our own money. When we take out a car loan or a home loan from the bank, the funds are restricted to that specific use. We purchase a certificate of deposit (CD) and are charged a penalty if we need to access that money before the term is up. If money is put into a qualified plan, we don't have control of that money until we reach a certain age or we pay a penalty for early withdrawal of our funds. When you look at the total amount of money you earn versus what you actually have left in your checking account, it's clear that you often don't have a lot of liquidity nor do you have a lot of control.

The issue of control is especially true when you put your money into a qualified plan such as a 529 College Saving Plan or a 401(k) plan. You are not in control. You are hoping that whoever is managing the fund is going to do a good job and that your money will be

---

1. Donald L. Blanton, *Your Circle of Wealth* (Covington, Louisiana, Mele Printing, 2004), page 27.

there when you want it. You are hoping that you'll have more of it when you need or want it, be it for college, retirement or any other purpose. You are also hoping the stock market will go up, not down, at the right time for your needs. And what if this doesn't happen and you lose money inside your qualified plan? Does the fund manager lose money? The fund manager may lose sleep but not money. The fund manager still gets paid, and the institutions still get their fees. You're the one who loses. Your money is at risk, not theirs.

When you look at the total amount of money you earn versus what you actually have left in your checking account, it's clear that you often don't have a lot of liquidity nor do you have a lot of control.

Liquidity, use, and control of your money are important factors in being able to withstand a financial crisis, a job loss, change in health, or a family emergency. Unfortunately, when these types of crises occur, lending institutions will typically not loan you money. Even the equity in your house may not be available to you. When you need cash (and regular cash flow) to pay your bills, it's not a good time to realize that you don't have easy access to funds without penalty or tax. Jason Zweig of *The Wall Street Journal* recommends taking "*an inventory of all your assets: stocks, bonds, your home, your business and anything else you own. Size up what it would cost, and how long it would take to turn each of them into cash.*"[2]

With a whole life policy, you have liquidity, use, and control of your money. You can have access to your cash relatively quickly just by signing your name on a loan request form. You don't need a job, W-2 statements, tax returns, or a good credit score to get access to your cash. If you need money for any reason, it is available to you with no penalty. It's that simple.

---

2. Jason Zweig, "The Intelligent Investor: Smart Money Takes a Dive on Alternative Assets," *The Wall Street Journal*, January 17, 2009.

Access to Credit

There are two aspects to borrowing money: 1) the interest rate that somebody else is going to charge you to use their money, and 2) qualification, that is whether you are even going to be able to borrow the money at all. These two aspects are affected by a number of factors, including your job history, credit payment history, perceived income stability, FICO™ credit score and more. (FICO™ is a registered trademark of The Fair Isaac Corporation which developed the credit scoring system used to measure credit risk).

September 2008 marked the fiftieth anniversary of the first mass mailing of credit cards.[3] We now have a culture raised on five-plus decades of credit card use. Perhaps it's time to take a look at who is in control when we use our credit card.

I am not saying credit cards are bad. Credit cards can be an especially valuable tool if used wisely. What I *am* saying is that it is to your advantage to be aware that you are *not* in control of the interest rate, payment and general terms of use that govern your credit card.

Adam Levin, co-founder of the Consumer Information website Credit.com predicts, "*Credit line cutbacks will accelerate as credit companies try to shore up their finances before the new regulations take effect early next year* [2010]."[4]

"*The new rules aren't going to change that anytime soon,*" adds Greg McBride, Senior Financial Analyst with Bankrate.com, "*Consumers will have to brace themselves for higher fees, higher rates, and lower lines going forward, and that applies to those with good credit scores as well as bad.*"[5]

"A bank is a place that will lend you money if you can prove that you don't need it."

—BOB HOPE

"Banks don't lend their money. They lend the money somebody else left there."

—ADAM SMITH

---

3. Connie Prater, "50 years later, credit cards in the fabric of American life," *Taking Charge: a CreditCards.com Blog*, September 15, 2008, http://blogs.creditcards.com/2008/09/credit-cards-50th-anniversary.php (accessed August 12, 2009).

4. Cybele Weisser, "Could Your Credit Be Too Good?" *Time Magazine*, June 22, 2009.

5. Ibid.

Historically credit card offers have been easily available and can sound very attractive. Many families struggling with their cash flow will try to take advantage of credit card offers to access more money. Accumulating credit card debt can put additional emotional and financial strain on the family. Credit card debt can also make it difficult and expensive for the family to get any type of medium to long-term credit, including a home loan.

When you have a participating whole life policy, you have a built-in credit facility. You don't need to have a job or provide pay stubs to take out a loan. In fact, you don't need to have good credit at all because you don't have to qualify to borrow against your own money. Remember, the cash value of a whole life policy *is your money.* All you have to do is send the insurance company your loan request form, and a check will come in the mail. Sometimes if the amount you want is below a certain threshold value, in some cases, $3,000 to $5,000, you can receive a loan against your policy with just a phone call: "Hi, how are you? I'd like my money. Could you please send it to me?" The insurance representative will say, "Yes, where would you like it sent?" This is the loan process. There are no fees and no need to get approved. Compare this process to sitting down with a loan representative at your local financial institution.

I just spoke with a client who hadn't missed a payment on her credit card for more than six years. She had stellar credit! Then a payment was one day late, and her interest rate went from around 7% (which is extremely good for a credit card) to greater than 20%! My client called the credit card company and they said, "Sorry. You were a day late, and now it's 20% on the entire outstanding balance."

With a whole life insurance policy, *you* determine the timetable as to when you repay your loans. *You* decide how often and for how long you are going to make payments. If you run into cash flow problems, you don't have to worry about making the payments by a certain date each month. There are no late fees or reports sent to the credit bureau.

A Credit Card Experience

Recently, I received a letter from my credit card company, a major U.S. bank. In effect, the letter said that while the bank deeply appreciated my business, due to a change of business practice, the fixed interest rate applied to balances on my credit card was about to change.

The letter went on to say that my new interest rate would be variable and "more in line with the bank's business practices." The interest rate schedules provided were confusing but after some examination the bottom line was that the interest rates increased dramatically. Now, I will be paying the U.S. prime rate *plus* a marginal interest rate determined by the credit card company. What this amounts to is 3.25% for the U.S. interest rate (as of August 11, 2009) plus the credit card marginal rate of 13.74%. So, for any balances on my credit card I will now be paying 16.99%. However, if I miss one payment, the interest rate on all balances increases to 29.99%!

Currently, the U.S. prime rate is the lowest rate since August 4, 1955.* With the prime rate currently so low, in my opinion, given my new credit card terms, the only way the interest rate on my credit card can go is up!!

If this is happening to me then I'm sure it's happening to millions of other folks. This unilateral power of the banks and credit card companies to change our credit card terms is the stranglehold that they have on us.

Of course, the rebuttal argument is that if you don't like the terms of a credit card then you can close your account. This is true. However, if I close my account, it reflects negatively on my FICO score because now the amount of available credit to me has gone down. (The amount of credit available to you is an important parameter in the calculation of how your credit score is calculated.) So it's a Catch-22. If I don't like my new interest rate and I cancel the credit card, then my credit score goes down. I am potentially in a no-win situation.

However, with a participating whole life policy, if I use my credit card and, for some reason, cannot pay the balance on time, I have a way to avoid high finance charges. What I do is take a loan against my whole life policy, pay off the credit card and then pay back my whole life policy *under my own terms and conditions*. Using the credit facility built into the whole life policy, I can escape the onerous interest rates and business policies of the credit card companies.

*"History of The U.S. (Fed) Prime Rate from 1947 to The Present," *Prime Rate History*, http://www.wsjprimerate .us/wall_street_journal_prime_rate_history.htm (accessed August 15, 2009).

You are in complete control of when you return your own money to the cash value in your policy.

The credit availability in a whole life contract is one of the most powerful aspects of the policy and is grossly underutilized. In my opinion, there is no better credit facility out there than using the capital in your whole life policy. You control when and how much money you will pay back. You are going to pay interest to the insurance company on the money you borrow against your policy. But on the flip side, you're getting dividends (if declared by the insurance company's board of directors) that can, if you so decide, offset part or all of the loan interest depending upon the policy. How much interest have you paid to banks or other financial institutions? How much interest have they given back to you? That's right, none.

The credit availability in a whole life contract is one of the most powerful aspects of the policy and is grossly underutilized.

I ask my clients if they plan on paying back the money they borrow. I haven't had one person say they're not intending to pay back the money they owe. So if you're going to pay back your loans why not use your own capital via your whole life policy and increase your own wealth in the process? The interest you pay to others is lost forever.

We can't control the global economy. We can't control the national economy, the regional economy, or even the local economy. The only economy we can control is our household economy. One of the best ways to control our household economy is to control who we owe our debt to, the amount of debt we have and under what payment schedule we repay that debt. Whole life takes that control out of the hands of our creditors and puts it in ours.

Tax-Favored Environment

Taxes are eating away at our wealth. Let's say you want to go on a trip. You book your flight and pay the fees, surcharges and taxes on your airline ticket. If you book your flight over the internet, you pay taxes on your internet service. As you go to the airport and gas up, you pay all kinds of taxes (federal, state, and local taxes) on the gasoline. If you are driving your own car to the airport, you paid a sales tax when you purchased the car. You pay taxes annually on the licensing of the car.

As you go down the road, you have paid road maintenance taxes, which are part of your income tax, your property taxes and the taxes levied on gasoline. You have a bite to eat at the restaurant in the airport, and you get charged a sales tax.

On your trip you decide to go for a hike to get some fresh air. When you get there, you have to pay a park registration fee or a park user fee. Fees are like taxes. You either pay a fee or a tax on just about anything you do.

"In this world nothing can be said to be certain, except death and taxes."

—Benjamin Franklin

When you come home from your trip, you get off an airplane and proceed to the parking garage to get your car. To park at the airport in Seattle, for example, wrapped up in your parking fee is the actual charge for parking along with an airport tax, a city tax, and a sales tax.

If you think that being in the 30% income tax bracket means that you only pay 30% in taxes, you are wrong. All the extra taxes and fees are paid *in addition* to what we pay every April in state and federal income tax.

You also pay taxes when you take your hard-earned income and invest it *at risk,* in a mutual fund (outside a qualified plan). For example, if you are fortunate and your investment has gone up when you sell it, you pay a tax on your gain called a *capital gains* tax. Conversely, when you sell the mutual fund or investment you get a tax deduction if it were sold at a loss. If you don't sell the mutual fund then you pay taxes on the distributions you receive from the fund each and every year.

The good news is with your money inside a participating whole life contract dividends are considered a return of premium and are not taxed while in the policy. This is very different from corporate dividends, which represent corporate growth and are taxed at the dividend tax rate.

Reduced Interest Paid to Others

A common observation I hear from clients when talking about policy loans is this: "If I take out a loan against my policy, I'm going to pay interest to the insurance company." This is true. But, since the cash value in your policy is serving as collateral for the loan, the cash value in your policy continues to grow, even when you take money out as a loan.

"You finance everything you buy—you either pay interest to someone else or you give up interest you could have earned otherwise."

—R. Nelson Nash

Another way to increase the total amount of your savings is to pay higher loan payments back into your policy. For example, if your insurance company charges 8% interest on a loan against the policy, set up a repayment schedule for yourself at 12%. The additional 4% per payment per month will pay off your loan earlier and help grow the cash value of your policy. In many cases this growth, over the years, will produce an increase in cash value equal to or greater than the interest you would have paid to other financial institutions. This return comes to you not just via additional capital (more cash value) but also in the form of an increasing amount of death benefit that grows within your whole life policy. This can only be achieved if the policy is designed correctly.

It's almost always better to borrow using your policy than from any other financial source. I say *almost* because there are some situations that are beneficial to take advantage of if you are able to borrow less expensive money (i.e., borrow at a low interest rate and favorable terms such as some interest-subsidized student loans). However, these situations are rare and require very careful review.

Borrowing money from yourself and then paying yourself for the use of this money is the concept referred to as Economic Value Added (EVA). We'll be talking more about the specifics of this concept in

Chapter 3, but essentially, when we pay ourselves back for using our own money we are recognizing that our money has a very real value that can be calculated.

The Economic Value Added concept helps us understand why we repay loans borrowed against our policy at a higher interest rate than the rate charged by the insurance company.

No Government Involvement

With qualified plans, the government can change the rules at any time. As one client remarked to me, the government not only owns the chalkboard, but also the chalk. For the younger people who probably haven't ever sat in front of a chalkboard (a little sign of my age), think of the government owning the whiteboard and the erasable marker.

This is the difficulty. The rules keep changing to fit the times, a new political agenda, or whatever the government wants to do. Changing regulations can end up inadvertently penalizing the folks who have made every effort to do the right thing. For example, despite citizens paying into the Social Security program for what they thought were an appropriate number of years, the government has already raised the age when you can begin collecting Social Security benefits. While past generations could enjoy full eligibility for Social Security at age sixty-five, everyone born after 1937 must adhere to a tiered eligibility requirement. If you were born in 1960 or later, you are fully eligible for Social Security benefits at age sixty-seven not sixty-five.[6]

The first baby boomers turned sixty-two in 2008 and will turn sixty-five in 2011. As the baby boomer bubble moves through their retirement age, do you think it's possible that the government will have to change other rules and regulations to meet the demands of our

---

6. James E. McWhinney, "Introduction to Social Security," *Investopedia.com*, http://www.investopedia.com/articles/retirement/06/socialsecurity.asp (accessed August 12, 2009).

growing elderly population? Tremendous financial stress will be put on the Social Security System with all the new applications for Social Security, Medicare, and Medicaid. Just these three programs alone will place a huge burden on the governmental system to distribute funds from the taxpayers' coffers.

While qualified plans are subject to the government's jurisdiction and changing rules, money in the insurance world is a private contract. This means that the insurance company cannot change the rules without you agreeing to them. It is that simple. You understand what the rules are, and that is the way it is for the length of the contract. Since it is participating whole life insurance, this contract is for the length of your entire life. You know what the rules are, and you know what you can and cannot do. It's defined by the private contract between you and the life insurance company.

Insurance for Life

It is easy to underestimate the value of insurability. I think there is a common belief that if you are breathing and alive, you are able to qualify for life insurance. The belief that you can get life insurance at any time because you are alive is a very, very big myth.

There are all kinds of reasons why a person might not be insurable. For example, if you have an excessive number of motor vehicle moving violations or citations for driving under the influence (DUI), you are not insurable because your risk is too high. If you have a health condition that is undefined or puts you in too high a risk category, you are uninsurable. There are quite a few conditions that make a person unable to obtain life insurance. Consequently, the sooner you own a participating whole life insurance policy, the better, because there is no way of knowing whether you will become uninsurable tomorrow.

One approach to using life insurance as a financial tool is to obtain a whole life policy on a child because, typically, they are insurable. They have not yet lived very long, and it is less likely that something has happened to make them uninsurable. Also, as we grow into the teenage years and early twenties, there are some things we do that, when we look back years later, we realize, quite frankly, weren't that

A Personal Story

I would like to share with you a very personal story about my family.

Happily, my mother just celebrated her eighty-sixth birthday and doesn't take any medication. Not a single pill.

However, in October 2007, my brother went to the doctor with a cough and was dead seven months later on May 26, 2008 at the age of fifty-four. He was a husband, father, a grandfather, an uncle and my only brother.

My sister went to the hospital with severe stomach pain at the end of August 2009. Twenty days later on September 14, 2009 she passed away at the age of fifty-six. She was a wife, mother, a grandmother, an aunt and my only sister.

I don't know if you ever heal from such a loss because I am just beginning my journey. At this point I must admit I think you slowly move forward with life because, for me, that is the only direction to go. The grief process is complex and ever so personal.

With a heavy heart I have also witnessed first-hand, with family and friends,

the multitude of emotions that occur when a loved one passes. No one can take away the pain but one thing can be done.

What can be done with love and vision is to own an adequate amount of life insurance. Life insurance will not in any way relieve the sadness of your loss but it will remove the worry and anxiety about money so that you can live. Donald L. Blanton refers to life insurance as a "love" not a "need" product because it fulfills, with love, the financial responsibility of the person who passed toward his or her loved ones who remain.

What a wonderful gift not to worry or stress about how you are going to pay your mortgage, the car payment or any other financial obligation. With no anxiety about money, you are afforded the time, space and resources to heal. You can take the opportunity to offer and commit to helping the rest of your family or friends in their healing process because they might need you and you might need them more than ever.

bright. It sounded good at the time, but depending on what those actions were, the result can be that you are uninsurable. For example, using illegal substances in your teen or college years can make you uninsurable later on.

When a person considers permanent life insurance, he/she typically has a number of thoughts. First of all, many people have the following attitude, "Nothing will happen to me. I'm healthy and I'm going to live a long time." This thought is often quickly followed by, "It's too expensive. I can't afford it." Another common thought is that "I don't need it because when I retire in my golden years, I will have my house paid off. I will have enough assets, and if something happens to me, there will be enough money to take care of my loved ones."

All of these justifications are often used to avoid facing our own mortality and, in some cases, our own fear that we are inadequately prepared to deal with an untimely, life altering event, be it a marriage, death, divorce, job loss, or illness that we or someone dear to us experiences.

Sometimes, due to a variety of life circumstances, we are not where we had hoped to be financially. This can feel discouraging and it may be tempting to procrastinate on taking corrective action. It can also be comforting to hope that our mutual funds will go up and to tell ourselves that we have time to recover our lost investment. So, like Scarlett O'Hara, we're not going to think about it today. We have to confront this type of fuzzy thinking, take a deep breath, face where we are, and move to develop a clear financial strategy for the rest of our lives.

Predictable Results

Where are you going to get the money to live in your golden years? Are you sure your money is going to be there when you are ready to retire? In the insurance world, you have predictable results. You know where your money is, and you know how it is growing. You know how to access it. You are in control.

You often hear the comment that one of the largest investments a person makes is the purchase of a house. Typically we don't have the money to pay cash for the house, so we have to take a loan from the bank. Many homebuyers choose a fifteen, twenty, or thirty year amortization mortgage versus a one, two, three, or five year amortization payment plan (such as an option adjustable rate mortgage, or ARM). Why is this?

People tend to choose the longer traditional fixed payment plan because:

1. It lowers their payments.

2. They value the *predictability* of knowing what their mortgage payment is going to be over the long-term.

Mind you, property taxes typically increase over time. So the overall total payment does creep up, but you know the mortgage payment is going to be the same for the next fifteen to thirty years.

Let's look at predictability from a savings perspective and think of a permanent life insurance contract as a thirty year, fixed mortgage that pays *you*. But unlike the mortgage, it's not just a thirty year contract; it's a lifelong financial instrument with guaranteed predictable results. The predictability is guaranteed for life. Let me repeat that, it is guaranteed for life! The whole life contract is built so the cash value *never* decreases over the life of the contract.

Why can I emphasize the word *never?* The cash value is guaranteed not to decrease as long as premium payments are made, no withdrawals are made (i.e. there is no permanent removal of money from the policy) and any loans are repaid to the policy with interest.

"An economist is an expert who will know tomorrow why the things he predicted yesterday didn't happen today."

—Laurence J. Peter

The best question to ask is "What is my risk in that mutual fund or investment?"

So why do people place their hard-earned money into stocks, mutual funds, or some other financial instrument that is correlated with the stock market? To get the best rate of return, right? We are always asking, "What rate of return am I going to get on this fund or investment?" Perhaps this is the wrong question to ask. Perhaps the question we really need to be asking is "What is my risk in that mutual fund or investment?" *Let me repeat that: We need to ask, "What is the risk of losing my money? Can I live with the consequences if I lose part or all of my money?"*

Guaranteed Insurability

One of the benefits that can be added to an insurance contract is the guaranteed insurability rider. As we discussed earlier in this section, there is a tendency to believe we can always qualify for life insurance. However, lifestyle choices, accidents and illnesses may all leave us unable to qualify for life insurance. A guaranteed insurability rider gives the policy owner the right to make additional purchases of life insurance on the insured without having to take a physical examination or show other evidence of insurability. Additions can be bought at stated times and upon specified policy anniversaries. The specific conditions of the guaranteed insurability rider vary between insurance companies.

With a guaranteed insurability rider, you can guarantee that, at specific times and policy anniversaries, you will be able to continue to buy participating whole life insurance policies on the same individual without proof of insurability. Having multiple, well designed, whole life policies on one person enables the policy owner to capitalize on the financial potential of the policies and optimize his or her wealth.

Guaranteed Cash Accumulation

A participating whole life policy can be used as a forced savings vehicle—one that meets the basic saving needs. With your money in a participating whole life insurance policy, your money is not in the stock market and is at minimal risk. There is no need for annual balancing or realigning your asset allocation. Once your money is inside a properly designed whole life policy, you have access to the cash value without penalty or tax.

We'll further discuss and illustrate the power of whole life as a forced savings vehicle in *Chapter 3*.

Creditor Proof—Protected Asset (in certain states)

The cash value and death benefit of your whole life policy may be an asset that is not available to creditors. In other words, depending on what state you reside in, the cash value in your life insurance policy cannot be accessed by creditors. However, if you borrow money against your life insurance policy or transact any other withdrawals, then this money may become available to creditors.

Points to Review

- Participating whole life insurance provides an effective and stable wealth-growing vehicle.

- With participating whole life, you make premium payments, which contribute to your policy cash value and the death benefit.

Continued next page

Points to Review *(continued)*

- Participating whole life has built-in credit availability.

- A participating whole life contract gives you liquidity, use, and control of your money.

- In a participating whole life policy, you pay fewer taxes and fees on your money as compared to many other savings and investment vehicles.

- Your money's grouth in a participating whole life policy is not correlated to the stock market.

- Whole life provides life insurance protection for your entire life regardless of changing health conditions.

- A whole life policy has a guaranteed minimum cash value.

- Whole life is easy to use and addresses many financial needs and wants.

Why is Life Insurance so Misunderstood?

Many people view life insurance as something that they personally won't get to use or receive a benefit. They see it as a necessary expense to protect their families because the money is paid out when they die and not before. Admittedly, viewed from this perspective, life insurance doesn't look particularly attractive.

"What we do not understand we have no right to judge."

—Henri F. Amiel

Let me frame life insurance in a different way. Imagine that it's like a chocolate bar. When the owner of the chocolate bar dies, his beneficiary gets the chocolate bar to eat after the funeral. Now why would a person want to buy a chocolate bar and never get to enjoy the benefit of it? No one wants to pay for the chocolate bar and never get to eat it. This is why term insurance is often purchased. It requires the smallest out of pocket expense that will provide some benefit to the beneficiaries. It's low cost because it's only in force for a clearly defined period of time and its purpose is not to provide any living benefits to the policy owner other than the death benefit.

But what if I could show you a way where you can buy the chocolate bar and throughout your life be able to smell it, eat it, and enjoy it while you are alive? You and those you love are able to enjoy the sweet taste of it together. Plus, the chocolate bar continues growing, so when your final day comes, those close to you get even more chocolate. Well, this is exactly what can be done with a properly designed participating whole life policy. When you realize that there are tremendous benefits to owning whole life insurance *while you are alive,* then you will understand why people get excited about buying this type of life insurance.

Costs

Some people say that participating whole life insurance is a poor choice because it is front-loaded with costs. Whole life insurance policies *are* front-loaded with the costs of the actual death benefit, administration, and agent commissions.

An article in the November 2008 edition of Consumer Reports, *Money Adviser,* stated that *"because most cash-value policies are front-loaded with fees, you would likely need to hold one for upward of fifteen years before the cash value exceeded the premiums you paid."* [7] This may have been true of the policy that the author referenced; however, a

---

7. "Where to find emergency cash: guidelines for tapping your assets without paying too much in penalties and taxes," *ConsumerReports.org*, http://www.consumerreports.org/cro/money/credit-loan/where-to-find-emergency-cash/overview/where-to-find-emergency-cash-ov.htm (accessed August 12, 2009).

properly designed whole life policy on a healthy applicant will usually cover its start-up costs and begin lifelong guaranteed growth in half that time or less.

To better explore the concept of front-loading let's take a look at an example of a whole life insurance policy as shown in Table 5.

Table 5	Whole Life Illustration[1]				
Policy Year	Maximum Annual Net Premium	Cumulative Net Premium Outlay	Net Cash Value[2]	Difference Between Cumulative Net Premium Outlay vs. Net Cash Value	Net Death Benefit
1	$12,533	$12,533	$7,373	$(5,160)	$1,100,513
2	$12,533	$25,066	$17,608	$(7,458)	$1,198,830
3	$12,533	$37,599	$28,957	$(8,642)	$1,311,032
4	$12,533	$50,132	$41,030	$(9,102)	$1,422,598
5	$12,533	$62,665	$54,717	$(7,948)	$1,533,935
6	$12,533	$75,198	$70,289	$(4,909)	$1,645,258
7	$12,533	$87,731	$86,781	$(950)	$1,756,522
8[3]	$19,975	$107,706	$109,872	$2,166	$1,930,865

Notes

1. Hypothetical illustration that does not represent a specific product available for sale.

2. **Net Cash Value** includes dividends which are not guaranteed and are annually declared by the company's board of directors.

3. In **Policy Year 8**, the maximum premium payment which can be made increases from $12,533 to $19,975. This increase occurs to account for the Modified Endowment Contract (MEC) Rule as governed by the IRS.

Comments/Assumptions

- Net Premium Payments: The premium contribution for Table 5 has been designed such that the maximum amount of allowable premium is paid into the policy on an annual basis. The maximum amount of premium payable varies with time as a result of the effect of the Modified Endowment Contract (MEC) Rule. The impact of the MEC on the maximum allowable premium payment is discussed in the text.

- All Net Cash Values and Net Death Benefit values listed in Table 5 assume that annual dividends have been paid.

In the first year, Year 1, you deposit (via a total premium payment) $12,533 to start the policy. This is the maximum amount of premium you can contribute. This premium consists of the following:

Example 2	**Whole Life Policy—Premium Components (as shown in Table 5)**

Whole Life Insurance (base premium required)	$ 4,975
Paid Up Additions (optional rider)	$ 7,483
Guaranteed Insurability (optional rider)	$ 75
Total First Year Maximum Premium	$ 12,533

Note that by starting the policy with $12,533, this creates an immediate policy cash value of $7,373 and a death benefit of $1,100,513. More significantly, by temporarily restricting your access to only $5,160 of your total premium (Table 5), you have instantly created an asset, payable without tax, of $1,100,513 by way of the death benefit. Some folks tend to downplay the death benefit, but remember this is real money coming to your beneficiaries that you didn't have before. You purchased this death benefit of $1,100,513 for your beneficiaries by agreeing to a temporary lack of use of $5,160.

Let's continue with this example to Year 8. In a well-designed policy such as this one, you've paid $107,706 in premiums and your policy's net cash value (money available to you to use however you want) is now at $109,872. So in eight years, you now have access to all the money you have paid into the policy. You can take a loan against the policy to use this money in whatever way you choose, or leave it alone. It's your choice. Plus, you've now created a separate line of wealth (the death benefit) that will be paid to your beneficiaries free from income tax in most cases. If you just stop and think about this, I believe you can begin to see the power of this type of financial vehicle.

Recently I was speaking with a colleague of mine, David Barr, in the Washington State area about the concept of front loading. He commented that front loading is all around us, and he is right.

Education is a prime example—talk about front loading! Look at the cost of college, university, graduate work, and even postgraduate work. Why do people go to college and beyond? Of course, there are many reasons. One big reason may be the desire to explore a passion and to develop themselves and their careers. Likely, many individuals also believe that their investment in education will last them a lifetime—not just a period of time, but a lifetime.

Most of us will readily make that front-loaded investment in education, whether a university program or vocational training, because we believe that we will reap the benefits of this investment in some way for the rest of our lives. How is a properly designed, participating whole life contract from a mutually owned life insurance company any different?

Finally, the up-front costs and capitalization time of permanent life insurance are often overestimated, causing "financial experts" to tout that age-old cliché: *"Buy term and invest the difference."* A properly designed participating whole life policy can achieve respectable returns on your initial premiums in far less time than many "experts" predict. The living benefits of whole life more than make up for the difference in the cost of insurance. If you're in doubt about this, take a moment to look at Table 5 again and witness the stability, cash availability and the lifetime wealth that you've created for your beneficiaries and their families.

Who's Using Whole Life as a Financial Strategy?

If the concept of using whole life insurance as a financial tool is new to you, you might think that it's new to the marketplace. It's not. Participating permanent life insurance is such a sure thing that banks purchase it on their employees as a way of securing capital.

Barry James Dyke, author of *The Pirates of Manhattan*, made the following observations:

> *"[O]ne segment of the nation's economy completely understands the economic value of high cash permanent life insurance as a golden asset. . . . Banks buy permanent life insurance by the tractor-trailer loads. Banks own so much life insurance that the cash values on their balance sheets actually make them look like life insurance companies unto themselves. . . . Five of the six largest banks in the world—Citigroup, JPMorgan Chase, HSBC Holdings, Bank of America, and the Royal Bank of Scotland (through its Citizens Banks)—own significant amounts of high cash value permanent life insurance. . . "*[8]
>
> *"Bankers have wholeheartedly embraced high cash value life insurance as a safe economic power tool and have found the product to be healthy for the bottom line. . . . The CEO [of a Midwestern bank] confessed to [his/her] advisor that the bank-owned life insurance was the bank's best performing asset."*[9]

As you can see, banks themselves place a tremendous amount of value on participating whole life insurance as a safe and hard-working asset. Dyke goes on to highlight what we can learn from their strategies:

---

8. Barry James Dyke, *Pirates of Manhattan* (Portsmouth, New Hampshire, 555 Publishing, 2007), page 148.

9. Ibid., page 149.

> *"The nation's banks as a group are arguably the strongest and most influential economic power in the United States, as they ultimately control the entire nation's money supply. They have chosen, with precision and scientific analysis, to invest a very large percentage of the bank's assets and critical reserves prudently into permanent life insurance, treasury bills, cash, and other high-quality liquid assets such as gold bullion. Banks are not investing in mutual funds [or] speculative stocks . . . ."*[10]

In reference to the above quote, and in light of our recent financial crisis of 2008 and 2009, I think it's worth taking a moment to talk about the problems banks faced during this time because it had nothing to do with their insurance policies as assets.

As you'll recall from our discussion of the difference between banks and mutual companies, banks in the U.S. operate using the fractional reserve system. This is a banking practice in which commercial banks are required to keep only a fraction of the money deposited with them as reserves. You can see that this makes banks critically dependent upon borrowers making their loan payments regularly and on time.

In 2008 and 2009, when folks started defaulting on their mortgages this put tremendous financial pressure on banks. When people stopped paying their loans, banks still had financial reserves, but due in part to the fractional reserve system, they began suffering from a shortage of available cash (liquid reserves) and a drop in consumer confidence which caused many folks to withdraw money from their accounts.

---

10. Ibid., page 154.

Life Insurance as a Personal Financial Strategy

So, as this section of the book comes to a close, it seems to be a good place to recap where we've been and where we are going.

In *Chapter 1*, *The Basics*, we touched on the status quo and some of the key assumptions and limitations of qualified plans such as the 401(k).

Chapter 2, introduced the fundamentals of life insurance and the specific components of participating whole life insurance. The important benefits of life insurance when used as a financial tool were presented. Some of the misconceptions and myths in the marketplace about whole life insurance and why they're out there were also explained.

Hopefully, at this point in time, you're beginning to consider that whole life insurance can serve as the cornerstone of your financial strategy. As you now know, banks and corporations have been using life insurance as a financial staple for a very long time.

Remember, an effective and appropriately crafted lifetime financial strategy will work in strong and weak economic times. A properly designed participating whole life policy can function as a simple and powerful financial tool for operating a secure savings plan as part of a lifetime financial strategy. It can be used as a stand-alone strategy or in combination with other investment vehicles and approaches.

In the next section, *Chapter 3*, we're going to look at using whole life as a personal financial vehicle for you and your family. We're going to focus on the power of whole life insurance as a forced savings vehicle. I'm going to compare savings for college using your whole life policy with another popular approach: saving using the qualified college savings plans.

A Lifetime
Financial Strategy

When we think of life insurance and whether or not we need it, we often rely on the conventional wisdom in the marketplace that says if someone depends on you financially, then it's likely you need life insurance. Consequently, we only think of life insurance for ourselves or perhaps our spouse or partner. Certainly, this is an important aspect of life insurance—to create an estate or asset to protect those who are left behind when you pass away. However, as introduced in *Chapter 2*, using participating whole life insurance can be much more of a financial powerhouse than this conventional thinking would have us believe.

In addition to owning participating whole life insurance on ourselves, one of the most powerful ways to use life insurance is to obtain a policy on a child. Remember, we're paying for an insurance policy on a child *not* because the child needs insurance to protect any dependents but because this is an excellent long-term financial tool and the sooner you start a policy the more powerful it can be.

Designed correctly and implemented carefully, participating whole life insurance can become part of a multi-generational family financial plan

Obtaining an insurance policy on a child is not something that we hear about in the marketplace or that is common practice. The reason you obtain a child's policy is because it can become part of the cornerstone of a multi-generational financial strategy that will benefit you, your child and his or her family. It's also important to note that, for the protection of children, most insurance companies also have underwriting guidelines other than health which must be met before an insurance policy will be issued on a child. These requirements vary between insurance companies but include such considerations as the amount of insurance coverage on parents, and/or grandparents.

With respect to policy ownership, a requirement of owning a policy on someone else is that you must have an "insurable interest" in that person. That is, the policy owner must have interest in the continued life of the insured. This is why a parent or grandparent can own a policy on a child or grandchild; and an aunt or uncle can own a policy on a niece or nephew.

By working together, parents and grandparents can create a legacy for their child(ren). Children and grandchildren own their part of this strategy by paying premiums and managing the policy once they come of age. Designed correctly and implemented carefully, participating whole life insurance can become part of a multi-generational family financial plan.

Your Greatest Gift to a Child

What would be the perfect gift to give to your child, grandchild, niece, or nephew that would remind them of your love for as long as they live? Participating whole life insurance is a gift with no breakable parts and no batteries required. It won't end up in the toy graveyard, will never become too small, or go out of style. It will endear you to the child for life and says "I love you" more than words do. It helps you teach the child financial stewardship and creates a lifelong pool of money for your child to realize every opportunity. It is a gift that helps make your child's lifetime dreams come true.[1]

This gift will provide a pool of money to pay for your child's college education, finance his or her first car and every car thereafter for a lifetime. This gift may stand with your child at the altar of marriage, help to welcome his or her first child, cover the down payment on a house, and provide protection for your child's future family.

Most importantly, the gift will set in motion a financial strategy that will last your child's lifetime and supplement your retirement and his or hers. It will be a financial strategy that will teach the valuable lifetime lesson of stewardship. And best of all, this gift will never be lost to the stock market or the government.

When you put all those things together, the word *priceless* comes to mind. Let's examine how the whole life insurance benefits we discussed in *Chapter 2* create a more advantageous lifetime financial strategy than any other financial instrument.

What would be the perfect gift to give to your child, grandchild, niece, or nephew that would remind them of your love for as long as they live?

Prevention of Capital Loss, Steady and Stable Saving

One of the first and most important advantages of using whole life is the prevention of capital loss. The cash value in your policy cannot decline unless you borrow against or surrender the money from your policy and refuse to put the money back and pay the interest charged. By using a whole life insurance policy as a financial vehicle, you have set yourself up for predictable financial results. Compare this to any mutual fund. How often have your investments in mutual funds lost money despite your continued regular contribution?

---

1. Jonhenri Ball, personal conversation, January 10, 2009.

A second advantage is tax-deferred growth. Money within the policy will compound over time.

Is using a well designed whole life policy a get-rich-quick scheme? Absolutely not. What a well designed participating whole life insurance policy provides is low risk, steady and stable growth.

Think of the participating whole life policy in this way. We all want to get to the top of our financial mountain and this is the switchback trail, not the rocky face climb. That's right, one switchback at a time, one premium payment at a time. However, unlike the white-knuckle, rocky face climb, we know absolutely, positively that we're going to get there. It's going to take a while, but aren't we in it for a lifetime? When you start this financial vehicle, you are putting your money in a whole life insurance contract for the long-term. It is just like any long-term savings plan for college or retirement you may have, but with significantly greater lifetime benefits and lower risk.

Lifetime Capital Pool for the Child and Parent

This lifetime financial strategy works by using one pool of money (our policy cash value), over which we have liquidity, use and control. It works because we employ proper management and responsibility to make our premium payments and to pay our policy loans back to ourselves, as we are the lenders of our own money. We borrow or access the money that we have in the cash value portion of our policy and then we pay it back, with "interest," to ourselves instead of to somebody else.[2] There are no additional fees.

---

2. This "interest" is not really interest. Rather, it is additional premium (capital) that has been paid into the policy that equals the interest that was being paid to the lender. This is the reason that it is adding to the cost basis of the policy. Source: R. Nelson Nash, *Becoming Your Own Banker™—The Infinite Banking Concept™*, (Birmingham, Alabama: Infinite Banking Concepts, fourth edition, 2000) page 62.

When we need to access money at any time, it will be there within the policy. We don't have to hope that the stock market and our mutual funds or 401(k) growth align with our personal circumstances. Knowing that we have immediate access to cash provides peace of mind and a sense of security that being on the stock market roller coaster just cannot provide.

One of the most powerful aspects of the whole life insurance policy is the availability to you and your family of a credit facility that doesn't require a job or someone else's approval to access. You are not dependent upon your credit score, banks and their loan officers, nor do you need to rely on credit cards or worry about changing credit card payment terms and interest rate hikes.

With this lifetime wealth building strategy, we are creating a lifelong capital pool for the policy owner and the insured. Your wealth is not continually eroded by fees and interest paid to others.

A final advantage to the whole life policy is that it is a safe place to put money when, at any point in your life, you experience financial gain.

Teach the Child Stewardship of Money

Let's think back a little bit. Who taught you how to handle money? I know parents try to teach their kids about managing money, either with an allowance for completing chores or just the ten and twenty dollars handed out on Friday or Saturday to go to the movies or buy a special treat.

But where did the parents learn about money to teach their kids? Let's look back a little bit further. Maybe they learned it from their parents, from the media, advertising, radio talk shows, and TV personalities.

My point is, we as parents are trying to teach our children the stewardship of money; yet we have had very little training ourselves.

We say, "You have to save for that." But what are we doing? We aren't saving. We see a commercial on TV or we walk into a store and succumb to the delight of buying on credit and owning something new instantaneously. We justify our expenses by convincing ourselves that we will save for the next twelve, eighteen, or twenty-four months, and we will have the money to pay off our debts. Then life happens. A year goes by and we haven't saved because other expenses came up. Just when we think we're getting ahead, the dishwasher breaks down, the car needs new tires, the furnace needs repair, transportation costs go through the roof. All these extra expenses creep in and our debt creeps up. How does this teach the stewardship of money to our children?

By implementing a whole life policy, talking with your child about its impact, and using the policy in a financially prudent way, you are teaching your child to succeed at an important life skill. By observation and by discussion, you lead your child to a place of financial independence and knowledge that most of us never reach.

Provide Protection for the Child's Future Family

Another great benefit of whole life insurance is that it is, lest we forget, life insurance! A properly designed participating whole life policy provides protection for your child's future family in two ways. As life insurance, it will provide for the family in the unfortunate event of the insured's death. But also, as a living benefit, the policy's cash value is available if money is needed during the child's life to pay for unanticipated expenses or loss of cash flow, such as in the event of a layoff or injury that would create economic distress. With whole life you can prepare your child's future family for any life event because your child has a lifetime wealth-building strategy, not just a collection of financial products.

> ## Points to Review
>
> - A single whole life insurance policy creates an approach for building wealth that will last for a lifetime.
>
> - Whole life creates a pool of capital that can be used by parents and/or the child for self-financing purchases without need for qualification or penalty for use.
>
> - Whole life is a good vehicle for teaching the child responsible use of money, including borrowing and repaying loans to him or herself.
>
> - Whole life provides life insurance protection and emergency access to cash for the child's future family.

Whole Life as a Forced Savings Vehicle

People save money for different purposes and to meet a variety of needs. We save to buy a car, a house, for retirement, for college, for medical expenses, for vacations or for a multitude of other purposes. We also use short-term savings vehicles, bank accounts, money market accounts, certificates of deposits (CDs), etc. as a place to hold our money and manage our cash flow requirements. We have our long-term investments in the stock market within our qualified plans. Think of each of these accounts as being a separate pot. With so many pots of money, it's often hard to get our money to work efficiently and therefor our return on savings and investments is lower than we would like. At the same time, our money might be at higher risk than we would like.

We hope that by having our money in different places we diversify our risk and this might be true. But usually, we have small amounts of money in our bank accounts and certificates of deposit as compared to the money we have in qualified plans such as our 401(k) and qualified

College Saving Plans. Unfortunately, as we've discussed, placing the majority of our money in mutual funds and stocks within qualified plans is risky. Based upon the past few year's performance, you can't be sure the money will be there when you need it or if it's going to be there at all.

What many people want when they put their money in mutual funds, or any place for that matter, is for their money to grow and be there when they need it. In this section, I want to highlight using a whole life insurance policy as a simple savings tool—one that meets the basic saving needs without taking any loans against the policy, without accessing the credit capability of the policy. That's right, no policy loans, nothing. Just what you'd hope for with any savings vehicle—to be able to put your money in regularly, leave it alone and watch it grow without the worry or anxiety that you will lose it. When we think about savings, most of us hope to save one million dollars. We look at this level of saving as a bit of a financial mile marker.

When we think about savings, most of us hope to save one million dollars.

I've designed three hypothetical participating whole life policies (Tables 6, 7 and 8) based on a female, age eight, nonsmoker, standard rated, with monthly premium payments of approximately $260, $360 and $500. If you start making monthly premium payments of $260 per month (Table 6), you're saving $3,131 annually. With monthly payments of $360 (Table 7) and $500 per month (Table 8), you're saving $4,357 and $5,976 per year, respectively.

These numbers are not extraordinary. This is the point. Contrary to what critics of whole life say, *you don't need huge contributions to develop a sound lifetime financial vehicle*. Contrary to what you might think or have read, there *is* a place to put money (other than a low-interest bank account) where your money can grow steadily without tax and with very low risk.

Let's take a look at Tables 6, 7 and 8 on the following pages. I want to point out a couple of important features of these policies. These are illustrated in each table and also discussed within the text.

Notes

1. Hypothetical illustration that does not represent a specific product available for sale.

2. **Policy Milestone:** At Age 13, and for all years in the future, the premium payment of $3,131 causes the Net Cash Value to increase annually by more than $3,131. For example: at Age 12, the Net Cash Value equals $12,824. With the premium payment at Age 13 of $3,131, the Net Cash Value equals $16,507; or $552 more than the previous year's Net Cash Value ($16,507 minus $12,824 = $3,683 minus $3,131 = $552).

3. **Policy Milestone:** At Age 16, 8 years after the start of the policy, the Net Cash Value exceeds the Cumulative Net Premium Outlay.

4. **Policy Milestone:** At Age 61, you have accumulated $1,041,922 in Net Cash Value plus you have a Net Death Benefit of $2,318,618 by paying only $154,073 in Cumulative Net Premium Outlay.

Comments/ Assumptions

Table 6	Whole Life as a Savings Vehicle starting with $3,131/year premium (approximately $260/month)[1]			
Age of Insured	Net Premium	Cumulative Net Premium Outlay	Net Cash Value	Net Death Benefit
8	$3,131	$3,131	$1,712	$273,335
10	$3,131	$9,393	$6,767	$322,151
12	$3,131	$15,655	$12,824	$373,845
13[2]	$3,131	$18,785	$16,507	$399,692
14	$3,131	$21,916	$20,410	$425,531
16[3]	$3,194	$28,304	$29,110	$478,745
18	$3,102	$34,508	$38,923	$532,980
20	$3,102	$40,711	$49,849	$588,449
22	$3,102	$46,915	$62,217	$645,023
24	$3,194	$53,211	$76,340	$703,870
26	$3,012	$59,416	$92,228	$763,785
28	$3,012	$65,440	$109,893	$824,395
30	$3,012	$71,463	$129,802	$887,378
32	$3,012	$77,486	$152,315	$952,808
34	$3,194	$83,874	$178,101	$1,022,711
36	$2,783	$89,545	$206,412	$1,091,665
38	$2,783	$95,111	$238,232	$1,163,188
40	$2,783	$100,677	$274,168	$1,238,041
42	$2,783	$106,244	$314,750	$1,316,470
44	$3,194	$112,631	$361,355	$1,402,124
46	$2,441	$117,805	$412,584	$1,487,979
48	$2,441	$122,686	$469,858	$1,578,020
50	$2,441	$127,567	$533,963	$1,673,470
52	$2,687	$132,694	$605,848	$1,775,599
54	$2,705	$138,518	$686,680	$1,886,172
56	$2,091	$143,206	$775,489	$2,000,724
58	$2,091	$147,388	$873,586	$2,121,479
60	$2,091	$151,568	$982,562	$2,250,211
61[4]	$2,505	$154,073	$1,041,922	$2,318,618
62	$2,505	$156,577	$1,104,442	$2,389,162
64	$2,515	$161,606	$1,239,770	$2,537,003
65	$2,515	$164,121	$1,312,850	$2,614,460

- Net Premium Payments:
  The premium contribution for Table 6 has been designed such that the maximum amount of allowable premium is paid into the policy on an annual basis. The maximum amount of premium payable varies with time as a result of the effect of the Modified Endowment Contract (MEC) Rule. The impact of the MEC on the maximum allowable premium payment is discussed in the text.

- All Net Cash Values and Net Death Benefit values listed in Table 6 assume that annual dividends have been paid.

Notes

1. Hypothetical illustration that does not represent a specific product available for sale.

2. **Policy Milestone:** At Age 12, and for all years in the future, the premium payment of $4,357 causes the Net Cash Value to increase annually by more than $4,357. For example: at Age 11, the Net Cash Value equals $12,571. With the premium payment at Age 12 of $4,357, the Net Cash Value equals $16,977; or $49 more than the previous year's Net Cash Value ($16,977 minus $12,571 = $4,406 minus $4,357 = $49).

3. **Policy Milestone:** At Age 16, 8 years after the start of the policy, the Net Cash Value exceeds the Cumulative Net Premium Outlay.

4. **Policy Milestone:** At Age 55, you have accumulated $1,042,362 in Net Cash Value plus you have a Net Death Benefit of $2,783,172 by paying only $206,124 in Cumulative Net Premium Outlay.

Comments/Assumptions

- Net Premium Payments: The premium contribution for Table 7 has been designed such that the maximum amount of allowable premium is paid into the policy on an annual basis. The maximum amount of premium payable varies with time as a result of the effect of the Modified Endowment Contract (MEC) Rule. The impact of the MEC on the maximum allowable premium payment is discussed in the text.

- All Net Cash Values and Net Death Benefit values listed in Table 7 assume that annual dividends have been paid.

Table 7	Whole Life as a Savings Vehicle starting with $4,357/year premium (approximately $360/month)[1]			
Age of Insured	Net Premium	Cumulative Net Premium Outlay	Net Cash Value	Net Death Benefit
8	$4,357	$4,357	$2,055	$458,022
10	$4,357	$13,072	$8,775	$518,500
11	$4,357	$17,429	$12,571	$551,369
12[2]	$4,357	$21,787	$16,977	$584,317
13	$4,357	$26,144	$22,105	$617,404
14	$4,357	$30,501	$27,540	$650,581
16[3]	$4,357	$39,216	$39,495	$717,578
17	$4,357	$43,573	$46,219	$752,945
18	$4,357	$47,930	$53,331	$789,719
20	$4,357	$56,645	$68,699	$864,099
22	$4,357	$65,359	$86,108	$940,328
24	$4,357	$74,073	$105,875	$1,019,139
26	$4,357	$82,788	$128,248	$1,100,644
28	$4,357	$91,502	$153,370	$1,185,206
30	$4,357	$100,217	$181,645	$1,273,270
32	$4,357	$108,932	$213,616	$1,364,895
34	$4,357	$117,646	$249,692	$1,460,112
36	$4,357	$126,361	$290,336	$1,559,281
38	$4,357	$135,075	$336,171	$1,662,842
40	$4,357	$143,790	$387,933	$1,771,142
42	$4,357	$152,504	$446,382	$1,884,539
44	$4,250	$161,003	$512,044	$2,002,861
46	$4,175	$169,428	$585,874	$2,127,403
48	$4,175	$177,776	$668,746	$2,258,998
50	$4,282	$186,234	$761,608	$2,398,637
52	$4,282	$194,798	$865,496	$2,547,132
54	$3,723	$202,402	$980,247	$2,702,172
55[4]	$3,723	$206,124	$1,042,362	$2,783,172
56	$3,723	$209,846	$1,107,803	$2,866,781
58	$3,723	$217,292	$1,249,466	$3,042,141
60	$4,124	$225,139	$1,407,245	$3,229,856
62	$4,282	$233,703	$1,583,225	$3,431,227
64	$2,992	$240,451	$1,776,735	$3,641,547
65	$2,992	$243,442	$1,880,831	$3,750,999

Notes

1. Hypothetical illustration that does not represent a specific product available for sale.

2. **Policy Milestone:** At Age 12, and for all years in the future, the premium payment of $5,976 causes the Net Cash Value to increase annually by more than $5,976. For example: at Age 11, the Net Cash Value equals $19,045. With the premium payment at Age 12 of $5,976, the Net Cash Value equals $25,406; or $385 more than the previous year's Net Cash Value ($25,406 minus $19,045 = $6,361 minus $5,976 = $385).

3. **Policy Milestone:** At Age 15, 7 years after the start of the policy, the Net Cash Value exceeds the Cumulative Net Premium Outlay.

4. **Policy Milestone:** At Age 50, you have accumulated $1,049,961 in Net Cash Value plus you have a Net Death Benefit of $3,287,991 by paying only $242,979 in Cumulative Net Premium Outlay.

Comments/Assumptions

- Net Premium Payments: The premium contribution for Table 8 has been designed such that the maximum amount of allowable premium is paid into the policy on an annual basis. The maximum amount of premium payable varies with time as a result of the effect of the Modified Endowment Contract (MEC) Rule. The impact of the MEC on the maximum allowable premium payment is discussed in the text.

- All Net Cash Values and Net Death Benefit values listed in Table 8 assume that annual dividends have been paid.

Table 8	Whole Life as a Savings Vehicle starting with $5,976/year premium (approximately $500/month)[1]			
Age of Insured	Net Premium	Cumulative Net Premium Outlay	Net Cash Value	Net Death Benefit
8	$5,976	$5,976	$3,434	$521,819
10	$5,976	$17,928	$13,443	$619,382
11	$5,976	$23,904	$19,045	$670,903
12[2]	$5,976	$29,879	$25,406	$722,334
14	$5,976	$41,831	$40,329	$825,175
15[3]	$6,174	$48,005	$48,634	$878,806
16	$6,174	$54,178	$57,591	$932,471
18	$5,921	$66,020	$76,895	$1,040,096
20	$5,921	$77,862	$98,395	$1,150,041
22	$5,921	$89,704	$122,731	$1,262,095
24	$6,174	$101,798	$150,587	$1,379,092
26	$5,731	$113,702	$181,915	$1,498,050
28	$5,731	$125,164	$216,662	$1,617,711
30	$5,731	$136,626	$255,833	$1,742,009
32	$5,731	$148,087	$300,126	$1,871,094
34	$5,911	$160,172	$350,771	$2,008,486
36	$5,306	$170,784	$406,293	$2,143,607
38	$5,306	$181,396	$468,918	$2,284,787
40	$5,306	$192,008	$539,645	$2,432,497
42	$5,747	$203,324	$620,243	$2,590,126
44	$4,837	$213,840	$710,307	$2,752,652
46	$4,762	$223,439	$810,678	$2,920,573
48	$4,762	$232,962	$923,351	$3,098,216
50[4]	$5,256	$242,979	$1,049,961	$3,287,991
52	$5,300	$254,028	$1,192,556	$3,492,623
54	$4,134	$262,438	$1,348,691	$3,702,476
56	$4,134	$270,705	$1,522,328	$3,925,646
58	$4,134	$278,971	$1,715,175	$4,163,539
60	$4,889	$288,792	$1,931,025	$4,420,731
62	$4,962	$298,714	$2,170,861	$4,694,621
64	$3,413	$306,324	$2,434,756	$4,981,090
65	$3,413	$309,737	$2,576,855	$5,130,461

Table 6, 7 and 8 illustrate that using a whole life policy for nothing more than saving money makes sense. First, as long as you make your regular premium payment, your money grows. You're not subject to a sudden drop in the value of your asset. Second, you don't need large sums of money to save one million dollars. Clearly, if you save less money ($3,131 per year, Table 6) versus $5,976 per year (Table 8) it takes longer to achieve a saving of one million dollars. However, all you've had to do is make regular payments and not worry about your savings.

There are two other important policy milestones that are key attributes of a well designed whole life policy, and are clearly illustrated in these three tables:

Whole Life Policy Milestone 1:

At a certain time frame in the policy (which varies according to its design), the cash value will increase by at least, if not more, than the total annual premium you pay—as long as you make the premium payment.

In Tables 6 and 7, at age sixteen, or eight years after the policy was started (at age 15 in Table 8, or seven years after the policy was started), the net cash value of the policies are increasing by more than the amount of premium paid. This increase in cash value is due to the accumulation of guaranteed cash value and dividends (which may be declared annually by the insurance company's board of directors).

Whole Life Policy Milestone 2:

At a certain time in the policy the net cash value will equal or exceed the net cumulative premium in the policy. At this time you now have recovered all the money you paid into the policy. You can keep this money within the policy (as shown in all three tables) or borrow against the policy and repay it. (*Chapter 4* deals in detail with the power of policy loans).

Don't forget that, in addition to the net cash value of your policy, you also have a growing death benefit. This is a real asset that will be passed on to your beneficiaries and will help them in their lives.

What is the Modified Endowment Contract (MEC)?

To counteract what was perceived as an abusive use of life insurance policies as short-term, tax sheltered, cash accumulation or savings vehicles, the U.S. Congress, in June 1988, passed legislation modifying the tax law definition of a life insurance contract. This legislation created a new class of insurance contracts referred to as Modified Endowment Contracts.

The basic difference between Modified Endowment Contracts and other life insurance contracts is the federal income tax treatment received during the insured's life. Certain life insurance distributions, such as loans against the policy, policy withdrawals and dividends, are generally not subject to income tax in a participating whole life insurance contract. However, when received from a Modified Endowment Contract, these same loans against the policy, withdrawals and cash dividends are in fact, taxable as ordinary income and in some cases subject to a 10% penalty. (The 10% penalty applies to distributions taken before age fifty-nine and one-half).

Given that amounts received from Modified Endowment Contracts are treated as income first and taxed as such, it is easy to appreciate why it is important to ensure that your participating whole life insurance policy does *not* exceed the Modified Endowment Contract requirements.

You'll notice in the examples and illustrations within this book that premium payments vary. This is due to the fact that the examples chosen show how taking advantage of the maximum premium you can pay into a policy affects your cash value. However, since we're so close to the MEC requirement, this requires slight changes in premium payment to ensure that the contract does not exceed the MEC requirement.

Economic Value Added

One final concept that is helpful in understanding how to manage your participating whole life policy as a financial tool is the concept of "Economic Value Added." The September 20, 1993 issue of *Fortune Magazine* included an article titled, "The Real Key to Creating Wealth." Shawn Tully, the author, summarized the Economic Value Added concept for corporations. Mr. Tully wrote that cash or cash equivalents (such as life insurance, bank accounts, etc.) have value and corporate management must include this value when they calculate the cost of using the corporation's own money (capital) for future projects.[3]

With respect to participating whole life insurance, Economic Value Added is an important concept to understand and applies to individuals in the same way as it applies to corporations. Just like the cash or cash equivalent assets of a corporation, your money also has a value when you use it.[4]

When you spend a dollar from your pocket, you are not only giving up that dollar but also all the interest that dollar could have earned for your entire life if you had kept it in an interest-bearing financial vehicle. In other words, the perceived difference of benefit

---

3. Shawn Tully, "The Real Key to Creating Wealth," *Fortune Magazine*, September 20, 1993.

4. Joe Kane, *Personal Economics Group*, personal conversation, July 2009.

between the two alternatives is the opportunity cost of one choice over the other.

Economic Value Added addresses the fact that, due to opportunity cost, the cost of your equity is worth something. Your money or capital has a very real value that can be calculated. The Economic Value Added concept helps us understand why we repay loans borrowed against our policy at a higher interest rate than charged by the insurance company.

Before you buy an item, save or invest your money, consider how difficult it has been for you to earn each and every dollar. Think about the fact that each dollar in your pocket has a value above the value of that dollar. When you spend that dollar you are giving up what that dollar could have made in an alternative financial vehicle. Consequently, you can consider that there is an opportunity cost associated with the choices you make.

Essentially, you want each dollar in your savings or investments to perform at their optimum ability. Your cash or cash equivalents have value and you must include this value when you think about using your own money in the form of a loan against your policy. Therefore, when you borrow from your policy, you must assign a value or interest rate for each dollar borrowed equal to the highest amount that dollar could have earned regardless of the interest rate charged by the insurance company. For example, if the insurance company charges you an 8% interest rate, then you need to assign a value to your dollar above 8%, such as 12%. The additional 4% difference between what you pay the insurance company as loan interest and your actual payment into your policy per payment is your personal Economic Value Added.[5] This additional money can be put into your policy as long as your policy has the capacity to accept it through paid up additions.

---

5. Joe Kane, *Economic Value Added—PowerPoint Presentation* (Dallas, Texas, Personal Economics Group, 2009).

The lesson to be learned from personal Economic Value Added is that it is important to respect the value of your money and your desired return on your principal. If you assume that the cost of using your own money is zero, then you will make poor decisions about how you spend or invest it.

College Plans and the Whole Life Policy

Up to this point, I've been discussing the whole life policy as a forced savings vehicle. Now it's important to consider the two major reasons for saving, college and retirement. We've spent a fair bit of energy looking at 401(k) plans with mutual funds. I think it's worth taking a little time to compare the traditional savings plans for college to see how they compare to the savings approach we've just illustrated using a whole life policy.

Many people choose to save for their children's education using a college savings account. One of the most common types of college savings plans is called a 529, named for the applicable section of the federal tax code. A 529 is offered in most states and usually includes savings with tax advantages.

In a 529 you invest pre-tax dollars, which are typically housed in mutual funds until your child begins to attend college, at which point you can pull the money out tax-free and use it to pay for qualified education expenses.

Though the tax advantage is an attractive feature, college savings accounts such as the 529 have some definite drawbacks. For example, what if your child chooses not to go to college, wants to attend college in a different state, or is able to get scholarships to fund his or her education? In some cases you're able to transfer the plan to another family member. You might be able to withdraw the money for nonqualified expenses, but that causes your earnings to be subject to state and federal taxes plus a 10% penalty. And as Linda Thomas of the *Seattle Times* points out, "The funds have to be used for education by the time the beneficiary turns thirty" to avoid the nonqualified use penalty.[6]

Why contribute to a savings plan that puts restrictions on your money? Think about it this way. You're putting money into an envelope. The government controls the flap on the envelope that allows you access to the money. You can use it for only one purpose and that's education. You're also putting your money at risk because you have to invest it somewhere, typically in mutual funds, and most people invest for growth. Therefore, you may be taking more risk than you should with your child's tuition. My question to you is: Is your 529 plan a college savings account or an investment plan?

Jane J. Kim of *The Wall Street Journal* points out that "the economic downturn is highlighting some serious flaws in 529 savings plans."[7] These flaws are related to risk exposure, which, during market lows, can cause you to lose a great deal of your 529 savings in the stock market. Greg Brown, a mutual fund analyst for Morningstar.com, notes that most of the popular 529 options had too much exposure to stock, which "for a child that's nearing college, [is] simply too aggressive."[8]

A prime example of this is the Oppenheimer Fund snafu in 2008. The Oppenheimer plans were considered 529 star players in safety and performance, and one of the nine Oppenheimer managed plans even made it to the Morningstar Best List the year before it crashed. Unfortunately, all of the Oppenheimer plans had tremendous exposure to what was considered, "*one of the worst bond-fund blowups of 2008.*" One of the greatest flaws, says Greg Brown, is "*that the Oppenheimer portfolios positioned closest to college were the ones holding*

---

6. Linda Thomas, "A Short Course on College Investment Accounts," *The Seattle Times*, September 2, 2007.

7. Jane J. Kim, "529 Plans: Ranking the Best and the Worst," *The Wall Street Journal*, April 23, 2009.

8. Greg Brown, "The Best and Worst 529 College-Savings Plans," *Morningstar.com*, April 23, 2009, http://news.morningstar.com/articlenet/article.aspx?id=287783 (accessed August 12, 2009).

the largest portions in these bond funds."[9] This particularly hurt those parents of college-bound high school graduates.

What Greg Brown stresses in his report is that the 529 plans have lost a tremendous amount of money. He specifically mentions the Oppenheimer funds, which were the poster child for managing 529s, because the firm currently manages nine separate college funds in five states. One fund lost 35% in 2008 due to management bets on non-agency mortgages.

The Illinois Direct Sold Bright Star College Savings Plan, an Oppenheimer fund which made the list of the best funds the previous year, experienced losses that were so unprecedented in mid-January 2009 that Illinois State Treasurer Alexi Giannoulias indicated that he was preparing to file a lawsuit against the Oppenheimer funds.

You should never gamble with money you can't afford to lose and just being in the stock market is a gamble.

The point of my stating all of this is that when you invest in 529s, you have limited liquidity, use and control of your money. You don't know if that money is going to be there, even if you put it in managed funds. You should never gamble with money you can't afford to lose and just being in the stock market is a gamble.

During the recession of 2008, a large group of parents begged the IRS for help and got a small break. You see, in a 529 plan, as per the IRS, it's possible to change investments and rebalance your portfolio only once per year. So as Eileen Ambrose reports for *The Baltimore Sun,* investors that "had made a change in their account early in the year [of 2008]—often the time families make adjustments—were unable to act again as stocks tanked in the fall."[10] Due to the severity of the recession, the IRS allowed investors to make just one additional change in 2009 (for a total of two), giving them one last chance to

---

9. Ibid.

10. Eileen Ambrose, "529 College Investors get Leeway," *The Baltimore Sun*, January 25, 2009.

shift their assets out of investments that were losing money. This small victory did very little to compensate for the huge losses that 529 plans, and all exchange-traded funds,[11] took during the fall of 2008. Parents of children nearing college age felt the worst pain as they scrambled to come up with a new way to finance their children's education.

This last example proves that the government can change the rules of the 529 plan at any point in time. How does the money at risk in the 529 plan coordinate with the rest of what is going on in your financial life? When you really start peeling back the strategy of getting liquidity, use and control of your money, a 529 plan is just like any other qualified plan containing mutual funds. You give up control to the money manager and the government with all kinds of penalties, restrictions, and unknowns.

With all the 529 plans available, some turned out to be more successful than others. In *The Wall Street Journal* report entitled, "Did Your College Savings Plan Blow Up on You?" Jason Zweig discovered a great deal offered from one bank in Ohio reporting that, "It boasts 'maturities' of up to twelve years at yields as high as 5%. . . . It's tough to beat a risk-free 5% return exempt from federal income tax. What a tragedy that more states didn't offer similar options before it was too late."[12]

The performance and security advertised in this "remarkable deal" was exactly what is achievable with a properly designed participating whole life policy. Plus, you get the additional money from the death benefit and can use your primary savings (cash value of the policy) for any of our child's expenses at any college or other life pursuit.

---

11. Exchange Traded Funds are an investment vehicle traded on the stock exchange much like stocks.

12. Jason Zweig, "The Intelligent Investor: Did Your College Savings Plan Blow Up on You?" *The Wall Street Journal*, March 20, 2009.

Prepaid College Savings Plans

There are two types of College Saving plans: (1) the savings plans, from which you withdraw your money as cash for qualified expenses like the 529 plan, and (2) the prepaid plans, which allow you to pay for tuition at today's rate and use it at a later date when costs are likely to be higher. Many states offer prepaid plans. In the State of Washington, it is called GET, Guaranteed Education Tuition.

There's great peace of mind knowing that your child's education is paid for. It is also hedging a bet against the rising cost of education. The GET program, for example, allows parents to purchase "units" which are redeemable for tuition, board, books, and other qualified expenses when the child attends college. According to the GET website, a year's worth of tuition is worth 100 units. The price per unit in May 2009 was $101, a more than $20 increase from a few months earlier. The cost per unit is rising fast due to anticipated rising costs of education and poor performance in the program's investments. Even so, according to *The Wall Street Journal,* "prepaid plans are seeing renewed interest as families anticipate sharp tuition increases."[13]

Though popularity of prepaid plans is on the rise, the GET is underfunded. As of March 2009, the GET's assets "amount to just 88.7% of future liabilities, the worst showing in the program's 11-year history" according to a *Seattle Times* report.[14] The plan is guaranteed by the state, but University of Washington president Mark Emmert worries that though the plan is "worth saving," it's important not to set a policy that will "keep the GET program solvent by making the universities and colleges insolvent."[15] Somehow state-guaranteed

---

13. Jane J. Kim and Melissa Korn, "More Families Move to Lock in Tuition Rates," *The Wall Street Journal,* December 9, 2008.

14. Nick Perry, "Proposed university surcharge won't affect GET," *The Seattle Times,* March 20, 2009.

15. Ibid.

prepaid plans such as the GET program will have to make some changes in investments, policies, or payouts to continue to fulfill their goal of making higher education obtainable for families in times of rising costs.

The prepaid plan is a great program that will likely maintain its ability to finance college education. However, what if you need the money due to family hardship or emergency prior to the child attending college? The last place you would want to go is his or her college education, but if you need the cash, you need the cash. What are the restrictions and penalties for getting access to that money? What if the child, for whatever reason, doesn't go to college? Then what are the options for getting your money out of this program? Why put all these restrictions on your hard-earned dollars?

Placing money in a specified-use vehicle such as the 529 stretches families' incomes thin during hard times, forcing many people to forgo saving for college. In fact, Jilian Mincer of *The Wall Street Journal* reports that *"while assets in 529 plans climbed to a record $111.9 billion in 2007, a growing number of providers have seen a drop in new accounts in recent months* [Spring of 2008]—*a sign that families are struggling to juggle college saving with rising mortgage, food and heating costs."*[16]

Instead of separating your lifetime financial needs and wants into isolated groups of money designed for only one specific use, a single properly designed whole life policy will allow you to save for your child's or grandchild's college education while allowing you access to cash without penalty.

---

16. Jilian Mincer, "Slowdown Reaches 529 Plans," *The Wall Street Journal*, March 6, 2008.

Points to Review

- In a participating whole life policy your money is not correlated with the stock market. This is not the case for mutual funds.

- In a whole life policy you have access to your money without penalty for lifetime expenses, which is not the case with mutual funds.

- You can use a participating whole life insurance policy to help save for college *and* supplement your retirement. You can use a participating whole life contract to save for any and all life events.

From Concept to Reality

Dr. Kevin J. Lasko

I am writing this letter to congratulate Dwayne on the information he has assembled in this book.

When reading this book, please keep an open mind and 'turn off' all the talking heads you see on TV telling you what to invest in or what the newest "hot sector" is going to be in the future.

This book is based upon a 200-year old concept with a cutting edge application.

First, I have no connection to any insurance agency or insurance group. I met Dwayne at a seminar and we discussed the concepts summarized in this book. In listening to Dwayne, I was thankful that I had participating whole life insurance policies on my children. However, after reviewing my existing policies, I quickly realized that they were not set up correctly for me. The policies emphasized the death benefit at the onset and de-emphasized cash value or the amount of capital (money) in the policy initially. This design constraint reduced my ability to maximize the money I put into the policy (a vital limitation you will understand after reading this book). After reviewing my family's finances and changing some spending habits, I started new participating whole life policies on my children based upon the concepts discussed in this book. This allowed my money to start to work maximally for me and ultimately for my future and my children's future.

A quick example: In 2002, I started a policy on my oldest daughter who was five years old at that time. The annual base premium had been paid each year. However, this policy had originally been designed without the ability to put additional money into the policy because a paid up additions rider was not part of the policy. Due to this limitation, I started a new policy on my daughter in 2008 and structured it as Dwayne recommends in this book. The difference in cash value between the two whole life policies has been amazing! Even though I have been paying into the original 2002 policy for over six years, the cash value in this original policy is almost equal to the whole life policy I started in 2008. The ability to put additional money in the newer, properly structured 2008 policy made all the difference in the world. I was able to increase the cash value of my 2008 policy in a much shorter period of time.

In closing, please do not think that only the dollar amounts illustrated in this book are the ones that will work. The financial status of each family is different. When reading this book, *look at the concept* and not the numbers. Figure out how this will work for your family based upon *your* finan-

Continued next page

From Concept to Reality *(continued)*

cial status and get a policy started! Understand that by having a policy in place, you have access to capital when you need it for purchases throughout your lifetime. You are able to utilize the same product for securing generational wealth for your children and grandchildren. It is truly amazing!

This is a product/process that, if set up correctly, will give you ultimate liquidity, use and control of your money. It cannot be rivaled in today's investment world.

Full and complete permission was obtained to use this testimonial. No compensation was provided.

Case Studies
The Power of Whole Life

Introduction

We've now come to the part of this book where theory is pretty much behind us. In order to understand the true power of whole life insurance, it's time to look at a series of case studies in which we use the whole life policy to fund various events in a child's life.

Case Study 1: Financing a car at age 16

Case Study 2: College education at age 18

Case Study 3: Wedding at age 29

Case Study 4: Parent's retirement

Case Study 5: Child's retirement

These case studies were developed to reflect real-life scenarios. The basic premise of the strategy outlined in this book is that life events will happen, some of which we can plan for, but many of which will be beyond our control. Also, at certain points in our lives, we typically need to pay out relatively large sums of money to finance our various needs and wants. Our challenge is to determine how we can best prepare financially to manage our lives for anticipated events such as college and retirement, as well as to prepare for those difficult times in our lives such as a loss of job or deteriorating health.

As I stated earlier, the only economy you can control is your own household economy. *Only you can take control of your finances and your financial future.* This path doesn't have to be hard or ridden with anxiety.

I want to re-emphasize that obtaining a participating whole life insurance policy on yourself or anyone in whom you have an insurable interest, such as your child, grandchild, niece or nephew, can open up the power of this financial tool to you.

When reading this book, please focus on understanding the concepts presented rather than the exact numbers. The details will vary depending upon the individuals involved.

Many insurance critics will caution you that a participating whole life insurance policy on a child is a waste of money. Remember, however, that we're paying for a participating whole life insurance policy on a child not because the child needs insurance to protect any dependents (at this time) but because this is an excellent lifelong wealth building strategy. By starting a policy on a child you harness the power of compounding your money (as shown previously in Figure 1). A child's policy allows you the opportunity to work together as a multi-generational team to finance both the child's life needs as well as your own. This approach creates a powerful financial tool which is stable and predictable in its ability to generate wealth for you and your family.

With respect to the case studies shown, remember that the dollar amounts used are only examples. The financial status of each family is different. When reading this book, please focus on understanding the concepts presented rather than the exact numbers. The details will vary depending upon the individuals involved.

I've started with premium payments of around $12,000 per year. I know this might feel like a tremendous amount of money if you are still viewing insurance premium payments as a non-recoverable expense or cost. They're not. Also, you may be doing the math questioning how you would contribute $12,000 to a policy *in addition* to your current financial obligations. Again, that's not the case. I want to make sure you keep in mind the following points as you work through the case studies:

- Participating whole life insurance policies are not all created equal. To be used as a financial tool, these policies must be designed and tailored to your financial situation and requirements.

- We traditionally think of insurance as a non-recoverable expense or cost. However, the purpose of this book is to show you how limiting this conventional thinking is. As I illustrated in *Chapter 2* (Table 5) and *Chapter 3* (Tables 6, 7 and 8), in a well designed policy, you can recover the total premium paid into a juvenile policy (via the policy cash value) within the first eight or nine years. On a reasonably healthy adult, the net cumulative premium and paid up additions can equal the net cash value within five to seven years. After this time, assuming you continue to make your premium payments regularly and on time, the cash value of your policy can grow at a rate in excess of your premium payment. This is due to the effect of dividend payments (if declared) and paid up additions.

- As illustrated in Tables 6, 7 and 8, you can start a financial strategy with much less than $12,000 per year. The power of participating whole life insurance is very real with premiums on the order of $3,131 per year, approximately $260 per month (Table 6).

- The money to fund a whole life policy can come from a variety of sources. Often, the money comes from a combination of cash from income and by slowly liquidating and transferring the money from other financial assets into the policy. Remember, it's a lifetime strategy!

- This approach can be a multi-generational strategy involving you, your grandparents and your children. You can also set up a policy on your niece or nephew. You and the members of your family can all derive a benefit from using the policy as is illustrated in the following case studies.

With the case studies presented in this chapter, I also want to clearly demonstrate the power of using a whole life policy by taking loans. Simply put, the more you use the credit facility of the whole life policy (while maximizing the paid up additions), the better it gets. Why is this?

As you flow more cash through your whole life policy, over time you recover the loan interest you initially paid to the insurance company via your paid up additions, dividends (if declared annually) and by means of additional death benefit. The key is to maximize your premium payments to the policy up to the limit of the MEC Rule. This means that to harness the complete financial power of the whole life policy as a financial tool, it's in your best interest to fund the policy to the maximum. By paying the maximum premium payment (as shown in the following case studies), you capture the maximum amount of paid up additions, which in turn cause the cash value and death benefit to increase.

The insurance term for paying your maximum premium is "overfunding" because you don't need to pay the maximum premium to keep your policy in force. However, overfunding is a great financial strategy because every time you put a dollar into the policy beyond what is minimally due to keep it in force, you increase the death benefit by more than the dollar you put in.

Also, at any time the mechanics of the policy can be changed so that premiums can be self-funded from either the net cash value or the dividends (if declared annually). When you choose the latter option, you can actually access and use the value accumulated in the death benefit while you are living.

Overview of the Case Study

We're going to take a look at five case studies with a participating whole life policy for which the insured is a female child. In these case studies, we'll examine paying for life events using the wealth building power of the whole life policy and policy loans.

All of the case studies in *Chapter 4* will be based on a single imaginary family with parents, Ben and Suzanne, and their daughter Jenny whom they insured at the age of eight. We'll follow the family through the growth of their daughter and their changing lifetime needs and wants.

Ben and Suzanne apply for insurance on their daughter, Jenny, when she is eight years old. The insurance company underwriters rate her as "nonsmoker, standard," which is how juveniles are rated.

There are three major parties to a whole life insurance contract. You'll remember the figure below from earlier in the book. I've reintroduced this figure here, as Figure 4, since this diagram summarizes this concept of policy ownership and it's worth taking a look at again. I've also discussed policy ownership in greater detail in this section.

Parties to the Whole Life Insurance Contract

- The Policy Owners—Suzanne and Ben (parents)

- The Insured—Jenny (daughter, age 8)

- The Insurance Company

The owner(s) controls the money in the policy and also controls the designation of a single or multiple beneficiaries. If the child does not prove responsible, does not go to college or proves to be incapable of proper stewardship of money then the policy owner continues to maintain control of the money. The insured doesn't have access to the money. No trusts are required; the child must earn the right to become the life insurance policy owner as determined by the current policy owner(s).

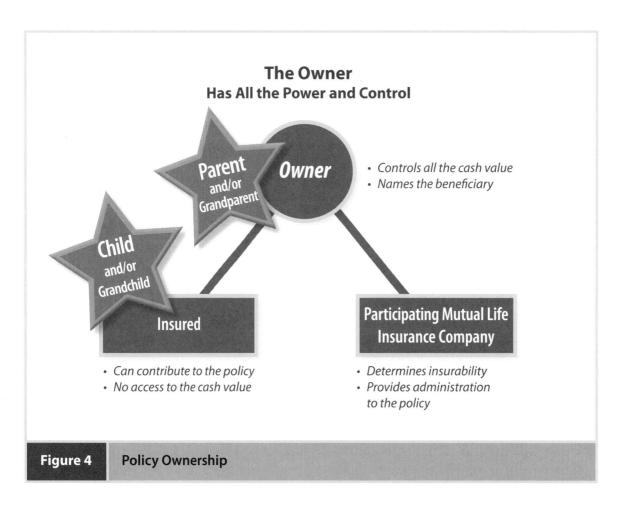

Figure 4   **Policy Ownership**

The insurance company will charge you an interest rate on any policy loan (in this case study it's 8%). Each insurance company determines the interest rate that they charge the policy owner for a loan against the policy so interest rates will fluctuate somewhat. However, the important point here is that you can pay the loan back on whatever schedule you choose. You can also choose to increase your payment amount on the loan to pay it off more quickly.

In the case studies presented here, I've chosen a specific loan repayment schedule depending upon the scenario we're discussing (e.g., car, college, wedding, etc). These are not the only repayment options available. Flexible loan repayment terms are a significant benefit of using a participating whole life policy as a credit vehicle. You decide the repayment terms because you're in control.

For each case study, I've included excerpts of this hypothetical illustration for your reference in the form of specific tables.

I'll be talking about each of the case studies in great detail. However, before I get to the specifics, I want to walk you through an overview of the policy. The hypothetical whole life illustration, showing all loans and repayments for Case Studies 1 through 5, is presented in Table 9.

The policy has been assumed to be funded to maximum capacity which means that at each opportunity the maximum amount of premium that can be paid has been put into the policy to the limit of the MEC Rule. (MEC limits are recalculated by the insurance company on a regular basis to ensure policies don't exceed the MEC amount). Due to the MEC Rule, funding the policy to maximum capacity means that the maximum premiums allowed will change over the life of the policy.

An additional note—you'll see the premiums vary as you study Tables 9 though 14. I've designed these policies for optimal financial flexibility and maximum growth. However, if you want the premium to be the same in all years, it's certainly possible to design the policy this way and still capture its power as a financial tool.

I've summarized the components of the maximum premium ($12,533) in Example 3. Although the impact of funding the policy to the maximum that it can handle is shown, to keep the policy in force the policy owner only needs to pay the base premium of $4,975 plus a $100 minimum paid up addition and $75 for the guaranteed insurability rider. Consequently, the minimum premium payment required to keep this policy in force is $5,150. You have the flexibility to pay any amount above the minimum, up to the maximum premium, each and every year.

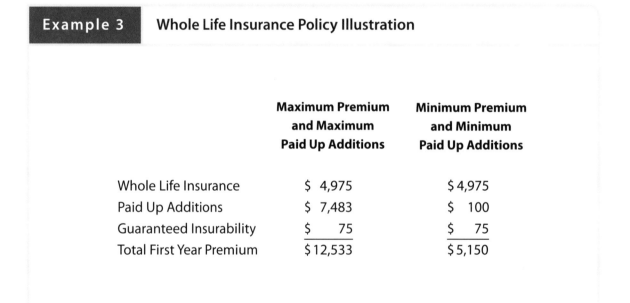

Example 3	Whole Life Insurance Policy Illustration

	Maximum Premium and Maximum Paid Up Additions	Minimum Premium and Minimum Paid Up Additions
Whole Life Insurance	$ 4,975	$ 4,975
Paid Up Additions	$ 7,483	$ 100
Guaranteed Insurability	$ 75	$ 75
Total First Year Premium	$ 12,533	$ 5,150

Let's walk through Table 9. The policy starts with the insured at age eight. We want to fund the policy to the maximum so each year we're paying the maximum net premium annual amount of $12,533. Notice that after seven years of paying into the policy (at age four-

Table 9	Whole Life Policy for Jenny With All Loans Illustrated (Case Studies 1-5)[1]						
Age of Insured	Net Premium	Cumulative Net Premium Outlay	Annual Loan	Cumulative Loan	Loan Payment	Net Cash Value	Net Death Benefit
8	$12,533	$12,533	$0	$0	$0	$7,373	$1,100,513
9	$12,533	$25,066	$0	$0	$0	$17,608	$1,198,830
10	$12,533	$37,599	$0	$0	$0	$28,957	$1,311,032
11	$12,533	$50,132	$0	$0	$0	$41,030	$1,422,598
12	$12,533	$62,665	$0	$0	$0	$54,717	$1,533,935
13	$12,533	$75,198	$0	$0	$0	$70,289	$1,645,258
14	$12,533	$87,731	$0	$0	$0	$86,781	$1,756,522
15	$19,975	$92,706	$16,200	$16,200	$0	$95,565	$1,929,571
16	$13,932	$115,110	$(7,854)	$8,346	$8,472	$124,101	$2,065,673
17	$13,343	$136,800	$(8,346)	$0	$8,346	$154,028	$2,199,964
18	$13,343	$145,143	$5,400	$5,400	$0	$171,487	$2,323,156
19	$13,343	$153,486	$5,832	$11,232	$0	$189,720	$2,446,531
20	$13,343	$161,829	$6,299	$17,531	$0	$208,993	$2,570,634
21	$13,343	$170,172	$6,802	$24,333	$0	$229,450	$2,695,357
22	$13,343	$143,515	$45,147	$69,480	$0	$213,526	$2,783,781
23	$17,880	$173,395	$(7,402)	$62,078	$12,000	$256,580	$2,963,575
24	$12,312	$197,707	$(7,994)	$54,084	$12,000	$296,872	$3,102,539
25	$12,312	$222,019	$(8,633)	$45,451	$12,000	$339,750	$3,243,809
26	$12,312	$246,331	$(9,324)	$36,127	$12,000	$385,509	$3,387,237
27	$12,312	$270,643	$(10,070)	$26,057	$12,000	$434,248	$3,533,253
28	$12,312	$294,955	$(10,875)	$15,182	$12,000	$485,850	$3,682,354
29	$12,312	$277,266	$33,615	$48,796	$0	$495,911	$3,790,039
30	$12,312	$309,586	$(17,705)	$31,091	$20,008	$559,992	$3,953,395
31	$18,358	$347,952	$(19,121)	$11,970	$20,008	$634,304	$4,155,622
32	$11,331	$371,253	$(11,970)	$0	$11,970	$697,736	$4,311,916
33	$11,331	$352,584	$32,400	$32,400	$0	$720,296	$4,426,341
34	$11,331	$323,915	$33,843	$66,243	$0	$733,382	$4,481,958
35	$11,331	$292,746	$27,030	$93,272	$0	$744,337	$4,488,385
36	$11,331	$261,577	$27,762	$121,034	$0	$755,851	$4,492,990
37	$11,331	$230,408	$28,536	$149,570	$0	$767,770	$4,495,742
38	$11,331	$199,239	$29,384	$178,954	$0	$780,335	$4,496,726
39	$19,975	$179,214	$27,484	$206,438	$0	$804,903	$4,537,288
40	$6,872	$146,086	$27,908	$234,346	$0	$817,540	$4,518,530
41	$4,823	$110,909	$28,716	$263,061	$0	$828,773	$4,490,209
42	$4,823	$75,731	$30,971	$294,031	$0	$840,457	$4,465,524

Continued on next page

Table 9 *(continued)*		Whole Life Policy for Jenny With All Loans Illustrated (Case Studies 1-5)[1]					
Age of Insured	Net Premium	Cumulative Net Premium Outlay	Annual Loan	Cumulative Loan	Loan Payment	Net Cash Value	Net Death Benefit
43	$4,823	$80,554	$(12,850)	$281,182	$0	$895,420	$4,478,473
44	$4,823	$85,377	$(11,852)	$269,330	$0	$953,801	$4,502,138
45	$4,823	$90,200	$228	$269,557	$0	$1,015,654	$4,564,438
46	$4,748	$94,948	$(452)	$269,105	$0	$1,081,214	$4,629,379
47	$11,590	$106,538	$(1,265)	$267,840	$0	$1,157,556	$4,720,554
48	$11,890	$118,428	$(2,363)	$265,477	$0	$1,238,625	$4,815,285
49	$11,890	$133,844	$(3,524)	$261,953	$0	$1,324,386	$4,912,680
50	$9,603	$148,189	$(4,822)	$257,131	$0	$1,412,731	$5,006,006
51	$3,723	$158,556	$(6,195)	$250,936	$0	$1,500,171	$5,084,942
52	$3,738	$169,145	$(7,503)	$243,433	$0	$1,592,476	$5,167,938
53	$3,752	$179,966	$(8,958)	$234,475	$0	$1,689,852	$5,255,142
54	$3,770	$191,011	$(10,491)	$223,984	$0	$1,792,701	$5,346,759
55	$3,789	$202,287	$(12,168)	$211,817	$0	$1,901,296	$5,443,078
56	$3,798	$213,799	$(14,027)	$197,790	$0	$2,015,735	$5,544,245
57	$3,822	$225,539	$(15,963)	$181,827	$0	$2,136,477	$5,650,545
58	$3,840	$237,515	$(18,098)	$163,730	$0	$2,263,778	$5,762,240
59	$3,847	$249,713	$(20,381)	$143,349	$0	$2,398,615	$5,880,023
60	$3,863	$262,282	$(23,401)	$119,949	$0	$2,540,992	$6,003,590
61	$3,879	$275,049	$(25,994)	$93,955	$0	$2,691,155	$6,133,186
62	$3,885	$287,996	$(28,752)	$65,204	$0	$2,849,488	$6,269,012
63	$3,899	$301,122	$(31,698)	$33,506	$0	$3,016,558	$6,411,366
64	$3,910	$314,066	$(33,506)	$0	$0	$3,192,840	$6,562,003
65	$4,975	$319,041	$0	$0	$0	$3,379,481	$6,756,917

Note

1. Hypothetical illustration that does not represent a specific product available for sale.

Comments/Assumptions

*   Net Premium Payments: The premium contribution for Table 9 has been designed such that the maximum amount of allowable premium is paid into the policy on an annual basis. The maximum amount of premium payable varies with time as a result of the effect of the Modified Endowment Contract (MEC) Rule. The impact of the MEC on the maximum allowable premium payment is discussed in the text.

*   All Net Cash Values and Net Death Benefit values listed in Table 9 assume that annual dividends have been paid.

teen), we have paid $87,731 in cumulative premium and our cash value is $86,781. Also, in addition to having access from age eight through fourteen to the cash value in our policy without a penalty or fee; we have a death benefit of $1,756,522, an increase of $656,009.

Case Study 1—Financing a Car at Age 15

At age fifteen, it's time to buy a car. The loan amount is $15,000 with loan interest of $1,200 (8% of $15,000). Therefore Table 9 shows a total loan at age fifteen of $16,200. At this same age, you'll notice that the premium payment increased to the maximum allowable amount of $19,975 (due to recalculation of the premium in comparison with the MEC Rule). Although this illustration shows that the parents pay this maximum premium, the life insurance policy could still be funded with the minimum premium amount of $5,150 (shown in Example 3).

During ages sixteen and seventeen, the parents pay the car loan back (shown in the loan payment column as $8,472 and $8,346). Notice that at age seventeen, the cumulative loan column shows a zero balance reflecting the complete repayment of the car loan.

Case Study 2—College Education at Age 18

At age eighteen, it's time for Jenny to attend college. Jenny attends college for four years, from eighteen through age twenty-one. During her college years, since she can get very favorable loan terms, Jenny takes an interest-subsidized student loan to pay for her college tuition, books and miscellaneous expenses. This four year student loan amounts to $40,000 ($10,000 per year). Jenny's parents (Ben and Suzanne) take a loan against the policy of $5,000 per year to help

Jenny with her living expenses. At age eighteen, you can see the loan against the policy equal $5,400 ($5,000 plus 8% interest of $400), as shown in the annual loan column. The cumulative loan by age twenty-one is $24,333.

At age twenty-two, Jenny wants to repay her interest-subsidized student loan and avoid the interest she would now start paying to the lender. Her parents borrow $45,147 against the policy to pay off the interest-subsidized student loan. Consequently, at this time (age twenty-two), the cumulative loan outstanding against the policy is $69,480.

From ages twenty-three through twenty-eight, Jenny's parents continue to maximally fund the whole life policy premium. Jenny however, now begins to pay back her college loan by contributing $1,000 per month to the policy ($12,000 per year). The repayment of the loan is shown starting at age twenty-three (in the Loan Payment column).

I want to take a moment and comment on this $1,000 per month that Jenny will now pay into her policy to repay the cost of college. You may think it is a lot of money for a college student to start paying after he or she graduates from college. You're right. However, remember that as well as repaying college costs, this same financial vehicle is Jenny's savings account and supplemental retirement account. By repaying the loan, she is increasing the policy's cash value and death benefit as part of her own forced savings plan. It's a multi-function financial approach. I've chosen a $1,000 per month repayment plan for this case study. However, if this is too much, the power of this financial approach is that *you get to choose your* repayment terms. Jenny can repay her loan at $200 per month or $500 per month or any amount she chooses.

Case Study 3—Wedding at Age 29

At age twenty-nine, Jenny is getting married. Although she has been responsible and paid $12,000 toward her loan repayment, at age twenty-eight, there is still an outstanding cumulative loan of $15,182. Notice, however, that the policy has a cash value of $485,850. At age tewnty-nine to pay for Jenny's wedding; Jenny's parents take out a loan against the policy of $30,000. The cumulative loan balance at age twenty-nine is now $48,796.

At age thirty-two, Jenny and her parents have paid off the wedding and the complete cost of Jenny's education. The policy has a cash value of $697,736 and a death benefit of $4,311,916.

Notice the power of the parents and child working together using the same financial vehicle. If the parents had put money away in a 401(k), they might not have accessed this money to help Jenny with her college or wedding. For her part, by repaying her college education loan back into the policy, these loan repayments caused an increase in the cash value and death benefit. Jenny's parents also have access to the cash value in the policy for any purchases they need or want to make during these years. It's a win-win strategy.

Case Study 4—Parent's Retirement

When Jenny is thirty-three, her parents start to borrow against the policy to supplement their retirement. Now Jenny takes over the premium payments of just under $1,000 per month, approximately $11,000 per year. Jenny can handle this premium payment because she has paid off her college debt and is already used to saving the $1,000 per month. Her parents borrow $400,000 against the policy over the next ten years—an amount which is not taxable because it is a policy loan. Jenny's parents do not repay the $400,000 loan back into the policy. However, because Jenny continues to pay the premium, the cash value of the policy continues to increase. When Jenny is age forty-two, over a period of ten years; her parents have borrowed a total $400,000 against the policy.

If you look at the cumulative loan column for age forty-two, you'll see a cumulative loan amount of $294,031. This number is less than the $400,000 that Ben and Suzanne borrowed against the policy. The cumulative loan outstanding of $294,031 is less than the loan amount of $400,000 because before Ben and Suzanne started to take loans against the policy to supplement their retirement, they changed the mechanics of the policy to apply the dividends received to reduce the amount of the loan. Consequently, dividends have helped reduce the overall amount of the loan to $294,031.

When Jenny is forty-three, her parents stop borrowing against the policy. Annual dividend payments (if declared by the insurance company's board of directors) are continuing to reduce the loan and Jenny continues to pay the maximum allowable premium.

Case Study 5—Child's Retirement

At age sixty-five, Jenny is ready to retire. Thanks to her parents and her own fiscal responsibility, she has $3,379,481 available to her in the net cash value with a net death benefit of $6,756,917.

We've finished with our overview of all the case studies. Now let's review the specifics of each case study.

Case Study 1: Financing a Car at Age 15

In this first case study. Ben and Suzanne are looking to purchase a second car to be used primarily by Jenny. They are deciding how they will pay for this car.

Instead of being subjected to lender financing options, Ben and Suzanne want to pay cash for the car. They're going to get the cash for the car by taking a loan against Jenny's whole life policy. They want their daughter to have a safe and reliable car, so they're estimating the purchase price to be around $15,000.

The section of the hypothetical policy illustration relevant to this case study is shown in Table 10.

Remember that from the start of the policy, when Jenny was age eight, until Jenny turned fifteen, Ben and Suzanne have been paying the whole life premiums regularly and on time. They have also chosen to fund this policy to its maximum capacity and therefore have been paying the maximum premium possible during this time. Consequently, by the time Jenny is age fourteen, the policy has a net cash value of $86,781 (Table 10).

When Jenny turns fifteen, Ben and Suzanne are going to take advantage of the available cash value in the policy by taking a $15,000 loan against Jenny's whole life policy. The insurance company charges interest up front for this loan; in this particular case, it's 8% ($1,200). So Ben and Suzanne's total loan against the policy with interest is $16,200 (Table 10).

Also, Ben and Suzanne decided not to pay any of the car loan back the first year. Remember, you have total control of your payment terms and conditions.

Just a point to note, even though in this case study, no loans against the policy were made until the policy was in its eighth year, loans can be borrowed against the policy much earlier. In fact, one of the most frequent questions I receive is, "When can the policy owner access his

Table 10		Financing a Car at Age 15[1]						
Age of Insured	Net Premium	Cumulative Net Premium Outlay	Annual Loan	Cumulative Loan	Loan Payment	Net Cash Value	Net Death Benefit
8	$12,533	$12,533	$0	$0	$0	$7,373	$1,100,513
9	$12,533	$25,066	$0	$0	$0	$17,608	$1,198,830
10	$12,533	$37,599	$0	$0	$0	$28,957	$1,311,032
11	$12,533	$50,132	$0	$0	$0	$41,030	$1,422,598
12	$12,533	$62,665	$0	$0	$0	$54,717	$1,533,935
13	$12,533	$75,198	$0	$0	$0	$70,289	$1,645,258
14	$12,533	$87,731	$0	$0	$0	$86,781	$1,756,522
15	$19,975	$92,706	$16,200	$16,200	$0	$95,565	$1,929,571
16	$13,932	$115,110	$(7,854)	$8,346	$8,472	$124,101	$2,065,673
17	$13,343	$136,800	$(8,346)	$0	$8,346	$154,028	$2,199,964

Note

1. Hypothetical illustration that does not represent a specific product available for sale.

Comments/Assumptions

- Net Premium Payments: The premium contribution for Table 10 has been designed such that the maximum amount of allowable premium is paid into the policy on an annual basis. The maximum amount of premium payable varies with time as a result of the effect of the Modified Endowment Contract (MEC) Rule. The impact of the MEC on the maximum allowable premium payment is discussed in the text.

- All Net Cash Values and Net Death Benefit values listed in Table 10 assume that annual dividends have been paid.

or her net cash value?" The answer is that it depends on the insurance company. Some insurance companies allow the policy owner to access the net cash value anywhere from thirty days to thirteen months after the policy is in force.

Now, let's take a closer look at how money moves through the whole life policy with snapshots of the policy at age fifteen, sixteen and seventeen (Examples 4, 5 and 6). All the numbers shown in these examples are sourced directly from Table 10.

Example 4   **Whole Life Policy—Snapshot at Age 15 (Table 10)**

Age 15—Premium	$ 19,975	Age 15—Policy Net Cash Value	$ 95,565
Loan*	($15,000)	Age 14—Policy Net Cash Value	$ 86,781
Owner's Net Cash Outflow	$ 4,975	Increase in Policy Net Cash Value	$ 8,784

The loan interest of $1,200 is not factored into this example. When the loan was taken against the policy the interest was automatically deducted from the policy's Net Cash Value.

Increase in Policy Net Cash Value	(Age 14 to Age 15)	$ 8,784
Owner's Net Cash Outflow	(Age 15)	($ 4,975)
Owner's Net Cash Increase	(Age 14 to Age 15)	$ 3,809

Age 15—Net Death Benefit	$1,929,571
Age 14—Net Death Benefit	$1,756,522
Increase in Net Death Benefit	$ 173,049

You'll see as we walk through each year of the policy in Examples 4, 5, and 6, that by using the whole life policy to finance the purchase of a car, Ben and Suzanne actually grow the cash value and death benefit within the whole life policy.

At age fifteen (Example 4), after paying the $19,975 premium and taking a $15,000 loan, the net cash value in the policy still increased by $8,784. Even after making the premium payment of $19,975 and taking a $15,000 loan against the policy to buy a car, Ben and Suzanne have $3,809 *more* cash in the policy at age fifteen than they had at age fourteen. Also, from age fourteen to age fifteen, the net death benefit *increased* by $173,049.

Example 5	Whole Life Policy—Snapshot at Age 16 (Table 10)

Age 16—Premium	$13,932	Age 16—Policy Net Cash Value	$124,101
Loan Payment	$ 8,472	Age 15—Policy Net Cash Value	$ 95,565
Owner's Net Cash Outflow	$22,404	Increase in Policy Net Cash Value	$ 28,536

Increase in Net Cash Value (Age 15 to Age 16)	$ 28,536
Owner's Net Cash Outflow (Age 16)	($ 22,404)
Owner's Net Cash Increase (Age 15 to Age 16)	$ 6,132

Age 16—Net Death Benefit	$2,065,673
Age 15—Net Death Benefit	$1,929,571
Increase in Net Death Benefit	$ 136,102

At age sixteen (Example 5), after paying the premium of $13,932, and making a loan payment of $8,472, the net cash value within the policy *increased* by $28,536. One year after taking the $15,000 loan against the policy, Ben and Suzanne have $6,132 *more* cash in their policy than at age fifteen. The net death benefit also continues to *grow*, increasing by $136,102 from age fifteen.

| Example 6 | Whole Life Policy - Snapshot at Age 17 (Table 10) |

Age 17—Premium	$13,343	Age 17—Policy Net Cash Value	$154,028
Loan Payment	$ 8,346	Age 16—Policy Net Cash Value	$124,101
Owner's Net Cash Outflow	$21,689	Increase in Policy Net Cash Value	$ 29,927

Increase in Net Cash Value (Age 16 to Age 17)	$ 29,927
Owner's Net Cash Outflow (Age 17)	($ 21,689)
Owner's Net Cash Increase (Age 16 to Age 17)	$ 8,238

Age 17—Net Death Benefit	$2,199,964
Age 16—Net Death Benefit	$2,065,673
Increase in Net Death Benefit	$ 134,291

At age seventeen (Example 6), after paying the premium of $13,343, and making a loan payment of $8,346 the policy's net cash value increased by $29,927 along with an increase in the death benefit of $134,291.

Let's take a look at what Suzanne and Ben have accomplished over this three-year period, starting at age fifteen through the end of age seventeen. First, Jenny has a reliable car. Second, over two years, Ben and Suzanne have paid back a $15,000 loan against their policy. (Remember, they chose not to make a loan payment the first year they took the loan against the policy).

Ben and Suzanne's total net cash outlay (including premiums and loan repayment) from the time they first took the $15,000 loan against the policy (at age fifteen) through age seventeen has been $49,068 ($4,975 plus $22,404 plus $21,689). However, by using their policy as a credit facility, over this same time period, Ben and Suzanne have helped their policy's net cash value grow by $67,247 ($8,784 plus $28,536 plus $29,927).

Suzanne and Ben have also seen an increase in the policy's death benefit of $443,442 ($173,049 plus $136,102 plus $134,291). So, despite taking a loan against the policy and paying it back with interest, when Jenny is seventeen, Ben and Suzanne have $18,179 ($67,247 minus $49,068) in additional cash *over and above* what they paid into the policy. They have also managed to repay a $15,000 loan on a repayment schedule designed completely in accordance with their needs.

To sum up, Ben and Suzanne have a car for their daughter and more cash than they started with along with an increase in the policy's net death benefit. This is the positive effect of self-financing your necessary purchases by using a properly designed participating whole life policy.

Case Study 2: College at Age 18

Ben and Suzanne hope that after graduating from high school, Jenny will want to pursue a higher education. At this point Jenny is now eighteen, the car loan has been repaid, and Ben and Suzanne have just finished cleaning up after Jenny's high school graduation party. Where are they going to find money for college? Table 11 presents the whole life policy illustration between the ages of eighteen and twenty-two.

Suzanne and Ben assume that Jenny can get a very favorable interest-subsidized student loan which she is going to use to pay for tuition, books and other expenses. However, she's still going to need money for living expenses. Consequently, Ben and Suzanne are going to borrow $5,000 per year from the policy over four years to cover the cost of Jenny's living expenses at the university. However, unlike the car loan which they paid back over two years, Suzanne and Ben are going to let these annual $5,000 loans (and the loan interest) against the policy accumulate. In fact, they're not going to make any loan payments at all.

This is one of the benefits of using a participating whole life policy as a credit facility: *you're in control of the repayment terms of any loan you take out of your policy.* Remember also that the parent is the policy owner and, therefore, has control of all of the money.

When Jenny goes to college for a four-year degree program, we will estimate her total college bill at $60,000. This $60,000 is divided between books and tuition at $10,000 per year and $20,000 in living expenses over the four years ($5,000 per year). To cover Jenny's living costs, each year for four years, Ben and Suzanne take out a $5,000 loan against the policy, accumulating $20,000 in policy loans. With the 8% interest on the policy loan, by Jenny's fourth year of college, the cumulative policy loan amount is $24,333. Jenny also obtained an interest-subsidized student loan of $40,000 ($10,000 per year) during her four years at college to cover the cost of books, tuition and other expenses.

Table 11	College at Age 18[1]						
Age of Insured	Net Premium	Cumulative Net Premium Outlay	Annual Loan	Cumulative Loan	Loan Payment	Net Cash Value	Net Death Benefit
18	$13,343	$145,143	$5,400	$5,400	$0	$171,487	$2,323,156
19	$13,343	$153,486	$5,832	$11,232	$0	$189,720	$2,446,531
20	$13,343	$161,829	$6,299	$17,531	$0	$208,993	$2,570,634
21	$13,343	$170,172	$6,802	$24,333	$0	$229,450	$2,695,357
22	$13,343	$143,515	$45,147	$69,480	$0	$213,526	$2,783,781

Note

1. Hypothetical illustration that does not represent a specific product available for sale.

Comments/Assumptions

- Net Premium Payments: The premium contribution for Table 11 has been designed such that the maximum amount of allowable premium is paid into the policy on an annual basis. The maximum amount of premium payable varies with time as a result of the effect of the Modified Endowment Contract (MEC) Rule. The impact of the MEC on the maximum allowable premium payment is discussed in the text.

- All Net Cash Values and Net Death Benefit values listed in Table 11 assume that annual dividends have been paid.

In this particular scenario, Jenny used an interest-subsidized student loan to fund a portion of her education instead of borrowing the total cost of her college education ($60,000) against the whole life policy. Since she was able to qualify and obtain a student loan of $40,000 *interest-free* over her four-year college program, it made sense to take advantage of an interest-free loan while she was in school.

Ben, Suzanne and Jenny have already discussed their financial plan for Jenny's education. They want to repay the interest-subsidized student loan in full by borrowing against the policy once Jenny graduates, at age twenty-two, just as the student loan repayment schedule starts. Using this strategy, Jenny and her parents are optimizing both exceptional interest-subsidized student loan terms and also the availability of credit within the whole life policy.

Depending on which college Jenny wants to attend, critics will say that $60,000 is a low estimate to fund a college education. This may be true. However, how many people have $60,000 saved for college? I'm sure a number of people have; but there are many more people who haven't, especially after the tough economic times in 2008 and 2009. *Again, focus on the concept being presented here more than the numbers.* You can substitute your own numbers based upon your personal financial and family situation.

To recap, as part their financial strategy to pay for Jenny's college education, Suzanne, Ben and Jenny agree to pay off the $40,000 student loan soon after Jenny graduates from college. They do this by taking a loan against the whole life policy of $40,000 at 8% interest. Because Suzanne and Ben already borrowed $5,000 over four years from the policy for Jenny's college living expenses and let this loan accumulate; when Jenny is twenty-two, there is now a total cumulative loan against the policy for $69,480 (Table 11).

Let's take a closer look at what has happened inside the policy from age eighteen through age twenty-two as Jenny and her parents have used the whole life policy to help fund Jenny's college education (Example 7).

In Example 7, over the course of Jenny's college education, Ben and Suzanne paid a total of $66,715 in premiums into the policy. Even with the cumulative loan of $69,480, the net cash value of the policy has grown by $42,039. After paying the policy premiums, taking out $60,000 in loans against the policy ($69,480 including interest), Suzanne and Ben have $39,274 *more* cash than they have paid into the policy. In addition, from age eighteen through age twenty-two the death benefit has grown by $460,625 (Table 11).

What happens after age twenty-two? As she and her parents discussed, Jenny wasn't required to make loan payments while she was at school so she could focus on her studies. However, when Jenny graduates and joins the workforce, she now has to pay for her college experience and repay her college loan.

Example 7   **Policy at Age 18 to 22 (Table 11)**

Total Premium Payments	$ 66,715
Increase in Policy Net Cash Value	$ 42,039
Cumulative Loan (including interest)	$(69,480)
Policy Owners Net Cash Increase	$ 39,274

The cumulative loan for Jenny's education is $69,480 (Table 11). Ben and Suzanne have decided to amortize their money at a 12% interest rate. Consequently it will take Jenny ten years at $1,000 per month ($12,000 annually) to repay her college loan. Why a ten-year loan? Student loans are typically amortized over ten to twenty years for smaller more affordable payments. However, Jenny will be motivated to make her payments because unlike other students who took out traditional student loans and are paying a normal financial institution, Jenny will eventually get all her college loan payments back and then some (via the net cash value in the policy) if she responsibly pays back the policy loan.

Ages 23 through 28

Before we launch into a discussion of using the whole life policy to fund Jenny's wedding, let's take a look at what has happens inside the policy from age twenty-three to age twenty-eight.

Over the period when Jenny was twenty-three to twenty-eight, Ben and Suzanne continued to make the policy premium payments. Example 8 shows the effect of policy premium and loan repayment over this period. Tables 9 and 12 (Case Study 3) illustrate the policy years for this time period.

As illustrated by Example 8, from age twenty-three to age twenty-eight, Ben and Suzanne have paid a total of $79,440, into the policy. Jenny has paid $72,000 into the policy for a total of $151,440 in payments into the policy. Yet from ages twenty-three to twenty-eight, the net cash value available in the policy increased by $229,270. When Jenny is twenty-eight, Ben and Suzanne have $77,830 (or 51.4%) more than what they paid into the policy. This increased policy net cash value is the effect of loan repayments back into the policy and dividends as declared annually by the insurance company's board of directors.

In addition to the cash value of the policy, during this time, the net death benefit increased to $3,682,354 from $2,963,575. This is an increase of $718,779.

Example 8	Policy from Ages 23 to 28 (Table 12)

Payments made into the policy from ages 23 through 28 (inclusive):

Age (of Insured)	Annual Net Premium	Jenny's Annual Student Loan Payments
23	$17,880	$12,000
24	$12,312	$12,000
25	$12,312	$12,000
26	$12,312	$12,000
27	$12,312	$12,000
28	$12,312	$12,000
Total	**$79,440**	**$72,000**

Net Premiums Paid by Suzanne and Ben	$ 79,440	Net Cash Value Age 28	$ 485,850
Jenny's Student Loan Payments	$ 72,000	Net Cash Value Age 23	$ 256,580
Total Cash Flow into the Policy	**$ 151,440**	**Increase in Net Cash Value**	**$ 229,270**
Increase in Net Cash Value	$ 229,270	Age 28—Net Death Benefit	$3,682,354
Cash Flow into the Policy	$ 151,440	Age 23—Net Death Benefit	$2,963,575
Owner's Net Cash Increase	**$ 77,830**	**Increase in Net Death Benefit**	**$ 718,779**

$$\frac{\text{Owner's Net Cash Increase}}{\textbf{Increase in Net Cash Value}} \quad \frac{\$ \ 77,830}{\$ \ 151,440} = 51.4\%$$ *(increase in cash above what was actually paid into policy in premium and loan repayment)*

Case Study 3: Wedding at Age 29

Jenny began working at age twenty-three, and now she is twenty-nine. Ben and Suzanne secretly hope that one day Jenny will marry somebody rich with his own whole life policy and that he'll pay for the wedding. But love is love, and however it turns out, they want her to be happy and have whatever type of celebration she desires. So Ben and Suzanne are prepared to pay for a wedding. For simplicity's sake, we are going to assume that Cupid will strike at exactly age twenty-nine.

Table 12 summarizes the policy years for this case study.

Wedding at 29

Jenny is twenty-nine and has decided to get married. To pay for Jenny's wedding; Ben and Suzanne are going to borrow $30,000 against their policy. They are also going to have Jenny stop making her college loan payment of $1,000 per month ($12,000 annually) for one year so that she can use this money toward her honeymoon and other expenses.

In looking at their financial situation, Ben and Suzanne also decide that they are not going to start repaying the $30,000 wedding loan right away. They are going to wait for one year. When Jenny reaches thirty they will begin to repay the $30,000 wedding loan. Remember, Ben and Suzanne are in control of the repayment terms for their loan, not a financial institution. Could you do this with your lender?

Suzanne and Ben create their own payment schedule for repaying the $30,000. They decide to pay $667.33 per month ($8,008 annually) over five years at 12% interest. In addition to the wedding loan repayment, from age twenty-nine through thirty-two, Ben and Suzanne also continue to make the premium payments into the policy which total $54,313 (Table 12).

Table 12		Wedding at Age 29[1]						
Age of Insured	Net Premium	Cumulative Net Premium Outlay	Annual Loan	Cumulative Loan	Loan Payment	Net Cash Value	Net Death Benefit
23	$17,880	$173,395	$(7,402)	$62,078	$12,000	$256,580	$2,963,575
24	$12,312	$197,707	$(7,994)	$54,084	$12,000	$296,872	$3,102,539
25	$12,312	$222,019	$(8,633)	$45,451	$12,000	$339,750	$3,243,809
26	$12,312	$246,331	$(9,324)	$36,127	$12,000	$385,509	$3,387,237
27	$12,312	$270,643	$(10,070)	$26,057	$12,000	$434,248	$3,533,253
28	$12,312	$294,955	$(10,875)	$15,182	$12,000	$485,850	$3,682,354
29	$12,312	$277,266	$33,615	$48,796	$0	$495,911	$3,790,039
30	$12,312	$309,586	$(17,705)	$31,091	$20,008	$559,992	$3,953,395
31	$18,358	$347,952	$(19,121)	$11,970	$20,008	$634,304	$4,155,622
32	$11,331	$371,253	$(11,970)	$0	$11,970	$697,736	$4,311,916

Note

1. Hypothetical illustration that does not represent a specific product available for sale.

Comments/Assumptions

- Net Premium Payments: The premium contribution for Table 12 has been designed such that the maximum amount of allowable premium is paid into the policy on an annual basis. The maximum amount of premium payable varies with time as a result of the effect of the Modified Endowment Contract (MEC) Rule. The impact of the MEC on the maximum allowable premium payment is discussed in the text.

- All Net Cash Values and Net Death Benefit values listed in Table 12 assume that annual dividends have been paid.

At age thirty, Jenny also resumes her annual college loan repayment of $12,000 annually. Consequently, the total annual loan payment into the policy consists of Jenny's student loan payment ($12,000) along with Ben and Suzanne's wedding loan repayment ($8,008) for a total of $20,008. Ben, Suzanne and Jenny make their annual cumulative loan repayment of $20,008 into the policy at age thirty and thirty-one.

What happens when Jenny is age thirty-two? Ben and Suzanne have repaid their loan while Jenny makes one final payment such that all outstanding loans are paid. Why? As you'll recall, Ben and Suzanne set out a five-year repayment schedule for their $30,000 wedding loan so it would seem that they should have more loan payments ahead of them.

What has happened is that Ben, Suzanne and Jenny set their own loan repayment schedules at a higher interest (12%) than was required by the insurance company (8% interest). By paying 4% higher interest on the outstanding cumulative loan amount both the college loan and the wedding loan were paid off much faster. Also the loan interest from the insurance company is calculated annually. Therefore the outstanding annual loan is reduced at a faster rate as compared to loans from other lenders.

Remember, the additional 4% difference in higher interest and loan payments that Ben, Suzanne and Jenny paid the insurance company is their personal Economic Value Added. The last couple of loan repayments they make into their policy are the return that they are paying themselves on their money (above the actual interest rate charged by the insurance company to borrow against the policy).

Savings via Whole Life—Jenny at Age Thirty-Two

Let's pause for a moment and consider how long the policy has been in force and the financial effectiveness of this policy. Suzanne and Ben started the policy on Jenny at age eight. After twenty-six years of the policy being in place (Jenny is age thirty-two), Ben and Suzanne have a cash value of $697,736 with a death benefit of $4,311,916 (Table 12). At age thirty-two, or after twenty-six years of the policy being in force, how much money have Suzanne, Ben and Jenny paid into the policy? The total amount of money that Ben, Suzanne and Jenny paid into the policy, including premiums and repayment of all loans, was $476,253 (Example 9).

Example 9	Policy from Ages 8 to 32 (Table 9)

Total Net Premiums (age eight to thirty-two) paid by Suzanne and Ben	$335,449
Total Loan Payments (all years and loans)	$140,804
Grand total of cash flow through the policy	$476,253

During the twenty-six years that the policy has been in existence, Ben and Suzanne have had liquidity, use and control of their money for whatever they needed or wanted. They have financed a car, college and a wedding. Normally, people think of insurance only as an expense. However, by paying their premium regularly and paying back their loans, Suzanne and Ben have created a stable and predictable financial asset. Do they care what the stock market is doing? No. Have Ben and Suzanne wondered or worried as to whether their money will be there when they need it? No. Are Ben and Suzanne happy? Yes!

Also, at age thirty-three, although Jenny has paid off her student loan, she now starts paying the policy premiums. Due to the MEC Rule, the maximum premium is now $11,331 (approximately $944 per month). Jenny, Suzanne and Ben have discussed this shift in premium payment responsibility and all agreed to it as part of the process of transferring the policy ownership to Jenny.

This is where the policy becomes an extremely powerful financial tool. *At age thirty-three (Table 13) the starting point of saving for Jenny's future is with a net cash value of $720,296 and a death benefit for Jenny's family of $4,426,341.*

Compare this situation to most students who, having just finished paying off student loans at thirty-two or thirty-three, are starting to save from zero, often with little or no life insurance. Is Jenny happy that she has been working with her parents utilizing a participating whole life policy? Yes!

Case Study 4: Parent's Retirement

Jenny is age thirty-three. Now it is Ben and Suzanne's turn to benefit directly from the policy! Table 13 summarizes the whole life policy for the years we're talking about in this case study.

Ben and Suzanne are going to borrow $400,000 against the policy with loans over the next ten years to supplement their retirement.

Table 13	Parent's Retirement[1]						
Age of Insured	Net Premium	Cumulative Net Premium Outlay	Annual Loan	Cumulative Loan	Loan Payment	Net Cash Value	Net Death Benefit
33	$11,331	$352,584	$32,400	$32,400	$0	$720,296	$4,426,341
34	$11,331	$323,915	$33,843	$66,243	$0	$733,382	$4,481,958
35	$11,331	$292,746	$27,030	$93,272	$0	$744,337	$4,488,385
36	$11,331	$261,577	$27,762	$121,034	$0	$755,851	$4,492,990
37	$11,331	$230,408	$28,536	$149,570	$0	$767,770	$4,495,742
38	$11,331	$199,239	$29,384	$178,954	$0	$780,335	$4,496,726
39	$19,975	$179,214	$27,484	$206,438	$0	$804,903	$4,537,288
40	$6,872	$146,086	$27,908	$234,346	$0	$817,540	$4,518,530
41	$4,823	$110,909	$28,716	$263,061	$0	$828,773	$4,490,209
42	$4,823	$75,731	$30,971	$294,031	$0	$840,457	$4,465,524

Note

1. Hypothetical illustration that does not represent a specific product available for sale.

Comments/Assumptions

- Net Premium Payments: The premium contribution for Table 13 has been designed such that the maximum amount of allowable premium is paid into the policy on an annual basis. The maximum amount of premium payable varies with time as a result of the effect of the Modified Endowment Contract (MEC) Rule. The impact of the MEC on the maximum allowable premium payment is discussed in the text.

- All Net Cash Values and Net Death Benefit values listed in Table 13 assume that annual dividends have been paid.

Example 10 shows the amount Ben and Suzanne take out each year as a loan against the policy. Starting when Jenny is age thirty-three, Ben and Suzanne's first year loan is $30,000. No income tax is payable on this $30,000 or any of the $400,000 because yearly withdrawals are taken as a loan against the policy.

It is important to realize that just before Ben and Suzanne start borrowing against the policy they change the mechanics of the policy. They deliberately modify the operating parameters of the policy so that any dividends paid to the policy will be directed toward reducing

| Example 10 | Policy from Ages 33 to 42 (Table 13) |

Age of Insured	Net Premium	Parents Supplemental Retirement Loan Schedule
33	$ 11,331	$ 30,000
34	$ 11,331	$ 40,000
35	$ 11,331	$ 42,500
36	$ 11,331	$ 42,500
37	$ 11,331	$ 42,500
38	$ 11,331	$ 42,500
39	$ 19,975	$ 40,000
40	$ 6,872	$ 40,000
41	$ 4,823	$ 40,000
42	$ 4,823	$ 40,000
Total	$ 104,479	$ 400,000

policy loans, thereby offsetting the total cost of the $400,000 loan against the policy.

Starting at age 33, Jenny begins to pay the premiums into the whole life policy. She has been used to making a $1,000 per month ($12,000 per year) payment for her student loan, so paying the $11,131 per year in policy premiums should not be a problem. She needs to save to supplement her retirement and this policy is the perfect spot for her money.

By the tenth year, when Jenny is age forty-two, Ben and Suzanne have taken $400,000 in loans against the policy which exceed the total premium of $335,449 that they paid into the policy. However, notice that, at this time, the cumulative loan amount is $294,031, not $400,000 plus interest (Table 13). The dividends paid into the policy loan have helped reduce the overall amount of the loan to $294,031. At this time, the cash value of the policy is $840,457 and the death benefit is $4,465,524.

Ta da! This is where the policy really starts to jazz. Follow the cash in Example 11. Over ten years, Jenny paid $104,479 into the policy

Example 11	**Policy from Ages 33 to 42 (Table 13)**

Net Premium Paid by Jenny	$ 104,479	Net Cash Value Age 42	$ 840,457
Cash Borrowed Against Policy	$ (400,000)	Net Cash Value Age 33	$ 720,296
Net Cash Flow Into Policy	$ (295,521)	Increase in Net Cash Value	$ 120,161
Age 42 Net Death Benefit	$ 4,465,524		
Age 33 Net Death Benefit	$ 4,426,341		
Increase in Net Death Benefit	$ 39,183		

while her parents removed $400,000. Yet, despite the $400,000 in loans against the policy, when Jenny is forty-two her parents still have $840,457 in net cash value to borrow against if they want (Example 11, Table 13).

Meanwhile, from ages thirty-three to forty-two, the policy's net cash value increased by $120,161 and the net death benefit increased by $39,183. The death benefit did not increase too much because Suzanne and Ben directed the insurance company to apply any dividends paid toward reducing the $400,000 loan (and loan interest) and not paid up additions.

Example 12	Supplementing Retirement with the Policy from Ages 33–42

Age (of Insured)	Parents Supplemental Retirement Loan Schedule	Withdrawal from 401(k)	Taxes To Be Paid Assuming 30% Tax Bracket
33	$ 30,000	$ 42,857	$ 12,857
34	$ 40,000	$ 57,143	$ 17,143
35	$ 42,500	$ 60,714	$ 18,214
36	$ 42,500	$ 60,714	$ 18,214
37	$ 42,500	$ 60,714	$ 18,214
38	$ 42,500	$ 60,714	$ 18,214
39	$ 40,000	$ 57,143	$ 17,143
40	$ 40,000	$ 57,143	$ 17,143
41	$ 40,000	$ 57,143	$ 17,143
42	$ 40,000	$ 57,143	$ 17,143
	$ 400,000	$ 571,428	$ 171,428

How does this retirement approach compare to mutual funds in a qualified plan (such as a 401(k))?

In Example 12, if your retirement money is in a 401(k), assuming a 30% tax bracket, in order to spend $400,000 in after-tax income, you will need to withdraw $571,428 in taxable income from your 401(k). That's right; at a 30% tax bracket you will pay $171,428 in taxes over 10 years.

Compare this to the strategy Ben and Suzanne employed using their participating whole life policy. By borrowing $400,000 against their participating whole life policy, because it is a loan, Ben and Suzanne do not pay income tax on the $400,000. Also, since this is a loan, this $400,000 amount does not count toward their overall taxable income. Over a ten year period, the amount of income tax saved is at least $171,428!

Example 13	Amount of Before-Tax Income Required at 30% Income Tax Rate

Before-Tax Income Required	$ 57,143	Savings Required in 401(k)	$1,428,571
30% Income Tax Rate	$(17,143)	4% Annual Withdrawal Rate	$ 57,143
Net Income Desired	$ 40,000		

The accepted financial premise is that you have to accumulate a large asset and only pull 4% a year so you don't run the risk of using it all up. With this rationale in Example 13, to get $40,000 after tax you need to have saved $1,428,571 in a qualified plan such as a 401(k), withdrawing 4% would provide you with a taxable income of $57,143. After paying the 30% income tax you would have an after-tax income of $40,000.

Again, let's compare the traditional rationale against the participating whole life policy. Instead of saving $1,428,521 within a 401(k), using their whole life policy, Ben and Suzanne will have paid $335,449 in cumulative premiums into their participating whole life policy at the time they start borrowing against the policy to supplement their retirement. Even after borrowing $400,000 against the policy, because Jenny has continued to make premium payments, Ben and Suzanne still have net cash value of $840,457 in the policy. This is the huge impact and financial advantage that Ben, Suzanne and Jenny have created by working together financially.

Over a ten year period, the amount of income tax saved is at least $171,428!

That's the tremendous power of the whole life policy. What is easier to do? Save $335,449 via premiums in a participating whole life policy or $1,428,571 in a 401(k)?

Case Study 5: Child's Retirement

This is our final case study. Table 14 presents data for the years from age forty-three to age sixty-five that we'll be discussing in this section. For the purposes of this case study, we're going to assume that Jenny, now married, has children. The cash value of the policy will be available for any other loans or emergencies. Money will be available to her without her having to qualify at a bank or borrow at high rates from a credit card company.

Regardless of whether Ben and Suzanne have given Jenny control of the money in the form of policy ownership or are continuing to manage the policy themselves, the cash value of the policy is available for all kinds of life events and emergencies. As the owners of the policy, Ben and Suzanne also control who will be the beneficiary. They can designate Jenny as the sole beneficiary, her family or possibly their church or a favorite charity.

Does Jenny really need to participate in any government or qualified plans? No! She has a turbocharged participating whole life policy. After all her and her parent's life events, the car, college, wedding, and Ben and Suzanne's supplemental retirement, in the fifty-eighth year of the policy (when Jenny is sixty-five), the policy has a net cash value of $3,379,481 and a death benefit of $6,756,917. Starting with a child's policy enables you to capture the tremendous power of compounding your money over fifty-seven years. I don't know of any other financial product that can match these results with the same predictability and benefits as a participating whole life policy. And the policy is still growing!

What is easier to do? Save $335,449 via premiums in a participating whole life policy or $1,428,571 in a 401(k)?

At age sixty-five, Jenny can borrow against the policy to supplement her retirement without paying the loan back just as her parents did to subsidize their retirement. With a net cash value of $3,379,481, Jenny will have plenty of money to live out her dreams in her retirement years and still leave a sizable legacy to her heirs.

If you want to look at the hypothetical illustration for ages sixty-six through ninety-five, you can find it online at www.Financial BallGame.com.

Table 14		Child's Retirement[1]						
Age of Insured	Net Premium	Cumulative Net Premium Outlay	Annual Loan	Cumulative Loan	Loan Payment	Net Cash Value	Net Death Benefit
43	$4,823	$80,554	$(12,850)	$281,182	$0	$895,420	$4,478,473
44	$4,823	$85,377	$(11,852)	$269,330	$0	$953,801	$4,502,138
45	$4,823	$90,200	$228	$269,557	$0	$1,015,654	$4,564,438
46	$4,748	$94,948	$(452)	$269,105	$0	$1,081,214	$4,629,379
47	$11,590	$106,538	$(1,265)	$267,840	$0	$1,157,556	$4,720,554
48	$11,890	$118,428	$(2,363)	$265,477	$0	$1,238,625	$4,815,285
49	$11,890	$133,844	$(3,524)	$261,953	$0	$1,324,386	$4,912,680
50	$9,603	$148,189	$(4,822)	$257,131	$0	$1,412,731	$5,006,006
51	$3,723	$158,556	$(6,195)	$250,936	$0	$1,500,171	$5,084,942
52	$3,738	$169,145	$(7,503)	$243,433	$0	$1,592,476	$5,167,938
53	$3,752	$179,966	$(8,958)	$234,475	$0	$1,689,852	$5,255,142
54	$3,770	$191,011	$(10,491)	$223,984	$0	$1,792,701	$5,346,759
55	$3,789	$202,287	$(12,168)	$211,817	$0	$1,901,296	$5,443,078
56	$3,798	$213,799	$(14,027)	$197,790	$0	$2,015,735	$5,544,245
57	$3,822	$225,539	$(15,963)	$181,827	$0	$2,136,477	$5,650,545
58	$3,840	$237,515	$(18,098)	$163,730	$0	$2,263,778	$5,762,240
59	$3,847	$249,713	$(20,381)	$143,349	$0	$2,398,615	$5,880,023
60	$3,863	$262,282	$(23,401)	$119,949	$0	$2,540,992	$6,003,590
61	$3,879	$275,049	$(25,994)	$93,955	$0	$2,691,155	$6,133,186
62	$3,885	$287,996	$(28,752)	$65,204	$0	$2,849,488	$6,269,012
63	$3,899	$301,122	$(31,698)	$33,506	$0	$3,016,558	$6,411,366
64	$3,910	$314,066	$(33,506)	$0	$0	$3,192,840	$6,562,003
65	$4,975	$319,041	$0	$0	$0	$3,379,481	$6,756,917

Note

1. Hypothetical illustration that does not represent a specific product available for sale.

Comments/Assumptions

- Net Premium Payments: The premium contribution for Table 14 has been designed such that the maximum amount of allowable premium is paid into the policy on an annual basis. The maximum amount of premium payable varies with time as a result of the effect of the Modified Endowment Contract (MEC) Rule. The impact of the MEC on the maximum allowable premium payment is discussed in the text.

- All Net Cash Values and Net Death Benefit values listed in Table 14 assume that annual dividends have been paid.

Case Studies: Summary

Throughout our lives, there are three major drains on our money: taxes, capital loss and inflation. We can control the first two of these factors with the right financial strategy. With the case studies in *Chapter 4*, we have examined, in detail, the power of participating whole life in saving and paying for some of the large predictable life expenses such as a car, college, a wedding and supplementing retirement.

It's important to understand that the core strength of using participating whole life is in 1) the prevention of capital loss, and 2) the compounding of your money over time. This approach to forced savings enables you to retain your capital and to benefit from its exponential compound growth over at least fifty to sixty years (in the case of a child's policy).

In walking through each case study, we've also examined how powerful using the participating whole life policy as a credit facility can be for managing our own money, reducing interest paid to others and limiting the amount of income tax we pay on our money.

This financial tool also empowers us to supplement our retirement without relying solely on a company pension plan or government programs, such as Social Security, which are all subject to change due to political and economic factors.

Wrapping
It All Up

My main mission for this book has been to introduce you to a powerful but misunderstood and underused financial tool, participating whole life insurance. As I stated from the beginning, I wanted to get you thinking about a long-term financial strategy for *your* life using participating permanent whole life insurance. I wish I had been introduced to this financial tool long ago. My financial journey would have been easier.

One of the major points of this book is that you don't have to accept the conventional financial message that is repeated to us *ad infinitum*. You can set yourself on a different path—one that enables you and your family to reach a level of financial independence, peace of mind and safety that you might have never have thought possible. To get to this point, though, requires a willingness to explore the new and the different. I ask you to keep your mind open to the possibility that there's more wisdom out there than the traditional strategy of investing and staying in the stock market no matter what. You don't need to lie awake at night hoping that somehow the stock market will recover in time for you to meet your financial wants and needs.

We've covered a lot of concepts within this book. I encourage you to take your time digesting the information I've presented.

I've spent a good bit of time in this book telling you that stock market investments are not the only option open to you as a financial plan. I want to re-emphasize here that I'm not suggesting you give up on the stock market, only that you temper your enthusiasm for greater returns with a sound savings vehicle and asset diversification. There's nothing stopping you from using a participating whole life strategy as the cornerstone of your financial plan while investing in the stock market or other assets. Indeed, I hope you've been able to see from the case studies that using participating whole life as a savings vehicle, credit facility, college savings plan and a supplemental retirement plan allows you to optimize your money while providing financial freedom that empowers you to do what you want.

What I want for you is that you make your financial choices with knowledge and a clear sense of your own financial direction. Remember, any financial plan that is based upon a hoped-for return in the stock market (or in any market, for that matter) is *not* a plan, it's a wish. An effective and appropriately crafted lifetime financial strategy will work in strong or weak economic times.

Many people worry about their money. They worry if they are going to have enough money to send their kids to college and save for retirement. Many people worry about where they will get the money to live on if they end up unemployed or sick. People also fear losing their money through poor investment choices.

Why live in fear and worry? Why do all that to yourself? With a properly designed participating whole life insurance policy, you can let go of all that fear and *know*—not hope—that the money will be there because it is guaranteed to be. A lifetime financial strategy with a participating whole life policy is easy to create and implement. It's predictable and safe. The money is available when either you or your child needs or wants it. Most importantly, all critical variables are within your control. If you have lived in fear of not having money when you need it, why pass those fears and worries on to your children when you can design a very simple contract to take care of them and their heirs for life? You can achieve peace of mind with your money.

The overarching goal of using a participating whole life policy is to develop and carry forward into the future a multi-generational financial strategy. After all the living benefits that this strategy has provided over the years, there is still a death benefit associated with this policy. When the insured grows old and passes on, the death benefit will be paid to whomever he/she has chosen as his or her beneficiary. Perhaps this will be his or her own children; however, it could also include his or her charities or church.

Who knows what the future is going to bring? Being prepared to handle changing life events and circumstances by understanding your financial situation and being in control of your money is a solid multi-generational financial strategy. By taking charge and eliminating unpredictable results and unnecessary cash outflow, you can grow and enjoy your wealth efficiently for your entire life. This is the power of participating whole life insurance as a financial tool.

What's **Next?**

Now that you have read this book, perhaps you're wondering, what next steps to consider. This is an important question. As I've stated in this book, not all participating whole life policies are created equal. In fact, there are significant variations in the power and flexibility of the whole life contracts offered by the different mutual insurance companies.

To develop a participating whole life policy that can be used as a financial tool and a lifelong strategy, a specific set of design criteria need to be met. Your current and future individual financial requirements are also a critical factor in designing a whole life contract that will work effectively for you and your family as a long-term financial tool. It is *absolutely not* the case that "one size fits all."

When you set out to consider starting a participating whole life policy as a financial tool, you will need to investigate both the qualifications of the insurance representative and the insurance company. In reality, almost anyone licensed to sell life insurance can obtain a participating whole life insurance policy for you. However, since a participating whole life policy will last you or your child a lifetime, you will want to know that it is properly crafted for this strategy. In addition, it is important that the insurance representative understand your personal financial situation and be familiar with your beliefs about money.

If you would like to pursue a conversation with an agent regarding your financial strategy, I would encourage you to consider asking him or her the following questions:

- Do they have a participating whole life policy themselves?

- Do they have participating whole life policies on their children?

- Are they using their whole life policies as financial tools?

- Can they speak clearly and specifically to the critical design elements that are necessary to craft a participating whole life policy so that is can be used as a financial tool?

- Do they exhibit ease and knowledge in discussing the various aspects of your financial situation with you?

- Can they answer your questions on participating whole life to your satisfaction and with clarity?

- Are they discussing this approach with you as a lifetime strategy?

- Is the agent structuring the policy to meet your particular financial situation and the appropriate protection for you and your family?

Since the participating whole life policy is a contract with an insurance company, in addition to finding a qualified insurance agent, it's also important to consider the corporate structure and financial strength of the insurance company.

Key elements to consider in evaluating an insurance company:

- Is the company corporately structured as a mutual company (whose owners are the policy owners) or a public company (where the company is owned by shareholders)?

- What is the financial strength and stability of the insurance company (including such parameters as its financial ratings [e.g., Moody's, Standard and Poor's, etc.] and capitalization ratio)?

- What is the history of dividend payments—over how many years has the mutual insurance company continuously paid its dividends?

A final comment—participating whole life is a powerful financial tool if the policy is designed correctly. So take your time to find an insurance representative who is knowledgeable and personally uses this approach. Make sure you fully understand your policy. Remember, acquiring a participating whole life policy is fundamentally a two-part process—you need the policy designed and structured correctly to function optimally as a financial tool and you need an agent committed to helping and teaching you how to use it over many years.

Is it Too Late for Me?

The simple answer is no. Since the case studies in *Chapter 4* focused on the power of a whole life insurance policy over the course of a child's life, you may be thinking that this strategy is too late for you and/or your family. You may be wishing you had known about the power of this financial tool much earlier, perhaps when you had young children. You might wish your parents had known about this approach.

One of the important aspects of this financial approach is that it has merit even if you are older, single, do not have children or grandchildren. My point is that if you are in your twenties through your seventies, if you or your children, grandchildren or nieces and nephews are insurable, you can still set up a participating whole life policy.

It's true that if you are older you won't get the exceptional benefit of decades of compound dividends on the cash value within your policy as we've discussed in the case studies. However, by shifting assets over time into your participating whole life policy you will be able to realize many of the other major benefits this financial approach enjoys. These benefits, as discussed in detail in *Chapter 3*, include having liquidity, use, and control of your money, using the policy as a credit facility, keeping your money in a tax-favored environment, achieving predictable financial performance, creating a strong savings vehicle and reducing interest paid to others. Remember, a participating whole life policy can be a strong financial tool at almost any age.

A final intangible benefit of this approach is simply the financial peace of mind you provide yourself and your family by removing the fear, anxiety and worry about your money.

About **the Author**

DWAYNE BURNELL, MBA has over 20 years of business experience encompassing the management of both small and large companies. Dwayne works with clients across the country. A deep passion of his is counseling individuals, couples and families on their financial strategy. Dwayne's focus is on reducing risk and creative financial strategies in order to manage and build long-term wealth.

Dwayne is co-founder of FinancialBallGame™, a financial education company dedicated to improving financial literacy and awareness. He is also accredited to teach a Continuing Education (CE) class for Certified Public Accountants (CPAs) called, "Life Insurance as an Asset Class."

In addition to financial coaching and training at FinancialBall Game™, Dwayne is actively involved in his community as a member of the Board of Directors of the Bothell Chamber of Commerce in Washington. He has also created and presented management and marketing seminars for the U.S. Small Business Administration (SBA) and Service Corps of Retired Executives (SCORE).

Dwayne's education includes a Master of Business Administration-University of Tennessee (Knoxville), and a Bachelor of Business Administration-University of Oklahoma (Norman).

Dwayne is looking forward to discussing the contents of this book with interested readers. During his career, he has been a speaker at numerous conferences and events. He welcomes the opportunity to speak to your group. Dwayne can be reached by telephone at 425-286-7298 or 800-266-2971 (toll free) and via e-mail at PeaceOf Mind@FinancialBallGame.com.

Registered Representative of Park Avenue Securities LLC (PAS), 20700 44th Avenue West, Suite 240, Lynnwood WA 98036. Securities products and services offered through PAS, 1-800-600-4667. FinancialBallGame.com is not an affiliate or subsidiary of PAS. PAS is a member of FINRA, SIPC.

Disclaimer

This publication contains the opinions and ideas of its author. It is intended to provide helpful and accurate information on the subject matter covered. This publication is not intended as legal, tax, insurance, investment, financial, accounting, or other professional advice or services. If the reader requires such advice or services, a competent professional should be consulted.

Although every precaution has been taken in the preparation of this book, the publisher and author assume no responsibility for errors or omissions. No warranty is made with respect to the accuracy or completeness of the information contained herein, and both the author and publisher specifically disclaim any responsibility for any liability, loss or risk, personal or otherwise, which is incurred as a consequence, directly or indirectly, of the use and application of any of the contents of this book.

The example organizations, products, people, and events depicted herein are fictitious. No association with any real company, organization, product, person, or event is intended or should be inferred. Any resemblance to real persons, living or dead is purely coincidental.

The author and publisher are not sponsored by any insurance company. Relevant laws vary from state to state. While this book seeks to provide the most accurate and up-to-date information available, this may change, become outdated or rendered incorrect by new legislation or official rulings. The strategies outlined in this book may not be suitable for every individual and are not guaranteed or warranted to produce any particular results. Readers should use caution in applying the material contained in this book and should seek competent advice from qualified professionals before making significant changes to their financial portfolios.

Insurance Disclaimer

The illustrations provided in this book are for educational purposes only. They are not intended to represent or guarantee a particular result. They are not intended as legal, tax, insurance, investment, financial, accounting, or other professional advice or services. If the reader requires such advice or services, a competent professional should be consulted.

The illustrations contained within this book do not serve to represent or promote a particular insurance company, agent or policy. Results will differ by state, insurance provider and agent due to specific contractual design requirements and relevant state laws.

Dividends are not guaranteed and may be declared annually by the insurance company's board of directors. Figures depending on dividends are based on the non-guaranteed dividend scale and are not guaranteed. Illustrations provided in this book assume that the currently illustrated non-guaranteed elements, including dividends, will continue unchanged for all years shown. This is not likely to occur and the actual results may be more or less favorable than those shown. Future dividends may be higher or lower than those illustrated depending on the company's actual future experience. For a complete illustration, see your insurance professional.

Loans on whole life insurance policy cash values are typically income tax free while the policy remains in force provided that it is not considered a Modified Endowment Contract. The policies, as shown, will not become a Modified Endowment Contract (MEC). The term MEC is designated under federal tax law. If a policy becomes a MEC, surrenders, withdrawals or policy loans will be taxed less favorably than for a non-MEC.

This illustration shows one or more paid up addition payments after policy year 10 that exceed the basic policy premium. The insured may need to provide evidence of insurability before the insurance company accepts payments in excess of this limit. The insurance products illustrated within this book may not be available in your state or from your preferred insurance provider. Premiums must be paid if the policy is to remain in force. The policy as illustrated may not be available to all applicants and premiums may differ based on health qualifications.